Some days from a hill diary

Scotland, Iceland, Norway, 1943–50

Adam Watson

Dedicated to Tom Weir for his inspiration and companionship on the hill

Publication of this book was aided by the generous sponsorship of Bert McIntosh of Crathes near Banchory in Scotland and McIntosh Plant Hire (Aberdeen) Ltd, Birchmoss, Echt, Westhill, Aberdeenshire AB32 6XL, www.mphltd.co.uk

Published by Paragon Publishing, 4 North Street, Rothersthorpe, Northants, NN7 3JB, UK

Clachnaben, Crathes, Banchory, Aberdeenshire AB31 5JE, Scotland, UK adamwatson@uwclub.net

ISBN 978-1-908341-48-8

Book design, layout and production management by Into Print
www.intoprint.net +44 (0) 1604 832149

Printed and bound in UK and USA by Lightning Source

Front cover. Looking from the Black Bridge up Glen Lui to the conical Derry Cairngorm (right) and Ben Macdui behind Carn Crom at Glen Derry, September 1950

Contents

Foreword

This book rests mostly on diary extracts from 1943–50 when I was 12–20, mostly about days when the aim was to climb or ski. I omit great detail on wildlife or snow-patches. Also I leave out a few over-frequent youthful excesses such as 'like the Himalaya' or 'terrific' views. Otherwise I kept the original writing, apart from creating paragraphs and punctuating sentences for readability. By its very nature, any diary is partly anthropocentric. I hope this does not intrude too much on readers' perception of the beauty of hill, weather and wildlife, or of the fine folk of the hills.

Acknowledgements

Ian Murray and I discussed some drafts by both of us. We used his computer for speech recognition, hoping to reduce typing, but results were inaccurate. However, I appreciated his interest and comments. The late Tom Weir generously gave me permission to reproduce photographs that he had taken and given to me. I thank Art Lance for enhancing two photographs.

Chapter 1. 1943

In early April 1943 at the top of Craigendarroch at Ballater, a cock capercaillie flew off through a fir-wood, breaking scores of twigs. At the month's end I found the nest of a song thrush with five eggs almost hatching, in the roots of a fallen tree at Brunthall Wood near Turriff. The parent, screaming and chattering, continually swooped at my head, swerving just before reaching it. The eggs were a lovely sky-blue, with jet black marks, in a cosy nest of dried grass lined with dried mud.

At the beginning of May I found three curlews' nests, each with four eggs, within half a mile of one other near Brunthall. One at Braefoot Loch contained two greenish eggs with brown blotches and two buff eggs with dark brown spots. Later the eggs were cold, and although hoodie crows bred here they left the eggs untouched. The second nest lay in rough grass, and the chicks did not reach the juvenile stage. The third nest was in growing oats. Three young passed the stage of straight beaks to become reddish-brown juveniles, and parents accompanied them through most of the summer.

A mute swan at Loch of Aboyne sat on its nest in May, and on July 1 she had six cygnets. At Braemar in July, jackdaws were abundant and hoodies fairly common, oystercatchers numerous on shingle along with some pairs of ringed plover, and curlews common on riverside marshes to the west. Hoodies nested in a birch-wood below the chapel and are said to eat many poultry chicks on crofts up Morrone. I saw ring ouzels in rocks at the top of Slugain glen, siskins fairly common in the larger gardens, and a redstart at the Linn of Dee. Two adult eagles and a juvenile sailed above Carn Crom and I watched two pairs of ptarmigan on Carn Crom.

A great spotted woodpecker nested in a tree at Turriff waterworks. On September 23 a woodpigeon's nest had two well-incubated eggs in a beech at Balquholly, and on October 16 a nest in a spruce at Brunthall Wood held two eggs far advanced in incubation. A woodpigeon nest in a beech hedge was used for the second year running at Beech Cottage near Brunthall. At Castleton of King Edward I saw a water rail, and many dippers on the burn.

Derry Cairngorm from Carn Crom, July 1943

AW at Mrs Macgregor's garden, Tomintoul croft above Braemar, July 1943 (photo Stewart Watson)

Chapter 2. 1944

Saturday 26 February. Snowstorm near Turriff

Morning opened with some sun and half an inch of snow on the ground. I cycled up to grandma's house at Beech Cottage near Brunthall. At about noon, wet soft snow started to fall and in twenty minutes changed to fine powdery dry flakes, accompanied by a west wind. Soon the short blizzard was over and I walked to Braefoot Loch. I saw a kestrel, several waterhens and reed buntings, a heron, and 70 wood-pigeons and 80 mallard feeding in Bruntie's turnip field. But I saw another blizzard coming, so sped back to the cottage. It was to last the rest of the day and into the night. From the window, I could just discern through blinding drift the hedge ten yards away. I have never seen anything like it and watched for hours. Returning from shutting the hen-house and getting a pail of water at the outside pump, I tripped over a paling, so thick was the blizzard. I wondered how wild birds were faring in such a storm.

Sunday 27 February

The Teuchit (lapwing) Storm has certainly come. In the field above Braefoot Loch there were 10-foot drifts, the ditch to the loch was chock-full of ice and snow, and the snow sparkling in the willows made one think it was fairyland. But it was not! The road to Turriff was blocked and I had to fight my way down, between the blizzards and ice storms. One furious but short (thank goodness) hail shower was so thick, along with severe drifting from the fields, that I could not see the road or my feet on the pedals, and next minute I fell off into a drift! Somehow I found a small shed where I sheltered till the brief storm was over, however.

28 February

Train and bus fail to get through to Turriff. A little more snow fell, and the wind changed to south-west and strengthened.

7 April. To Ballater

The weather was beautiful. In the garden at Turriff the hen blackbird laid her second egg, slightly larger than the first. I went to holiday at Ballater with Stewart and cousin Doug. Much woodland has been cut around Aboyne. On the Loch of Aboyne swam many coots and waterhens, a pair of mute swans and a flock of mallard. Some snow lay on Morven and Mount Keen.

At 5 o'clock I walked round the town, finding at the foot of Craigendarroch a rookery of 47 nests in old Scots firs. On shingle by the golf course I saw a pair of ringed plovers, hard to see as they ran over pebbles. They flew across the river with rapid flight.

8 April. Craig Vallich of Glen Muick

A sunny day dawned. At Ballater I decided to go to Craig Vallich. On the bridge across Dee, a stone tablet tells of three bridges erected but swept off by spates, and the remains of a wooden bridge and of a stone one are still there. At the curling pond, a mistle thrush had a nest with two eggs in a spruce. Soon I heard rushing water and came to a dam where two dainty pairs of grey wagtails flitted and a hen capercaillie flew from a tree. After a wade in the cool dam I walked through deep heather up the hill.

All the way up rose many pairs of meadow pipits, and several wheatears at a stone grouse-butt. In places the hill is boggy with rough grass. At a butt lay a dead sheep, on whose body a hoodie crow feasted. A hen merlin glided past and a golden plover whistled in high song flight, my first golden plover.

Many curlews flew in display. The bird flies a few feet above the ground, then rises steeply, glides almost to the ground and repeats the performance, each time uttering its liquid tremulous bubbling song. I saw many pairs of red grouse. All cocks had bright red combs and an almost black dress, but hens paler combs and brown dress. I noticed only one single cock. At 1600 feet I flushed a cock, and nearby a hen beside a shallow scrape almost hidden among heather.

Blue hares abounded towards and on the top, much tamer than our brown hares at Turriff. At 2000 feet I reached the summit. It was very windy, so I descended to a hollow with a shooters' shed to have a short rest. To the south stretched a great moor down to the Pollagach Burn and beyond to the Angus boundary. Were it not for the continual call of curlews and crowing of grouse, these hills would be among the loneliest. Suddenly a huge raven flapped from a rocky slope, to be joined by another. They sailed in spirals up 500 feet, and then one turned a somersault while the other barked hoarsely.

In the afternoon I walked round the golf course. At the edge, a belt of Scots firs has whins, broom and wild raspberry underneath. A fresh dead peewit with an orange belly lay here, and a flock of 45 oystercatchers rested on shingle.

10 April. Morven

Weather beautiful. Today I decided to climb Morven and left at 10. Cycling through Ballater, I noticed unusually many blackbirds and song thrushes, a pair of each in every garden, probably because of numerous bushes. Up Glen Gairn I saw peewits dashing about and separate pairs of oystercatchers. At Lary farm at 1400 feet there were many house sparrows. They are not at Luibeg at 1400 feet, but it has no cornfields.

On the moor a beautiful very tame cock golden plover ran in rushes at the road edge. When approached, it walked off a little, extremely well-camouflaged and uttering a soft liquid pipe. Two more flew over the burn, with a flight like ringed plover but quicker. Soon I reached the lodge in a mature conifer wood. From the grass there rose ten blackcocks. They flew across to a plantation to the east, magnificent birds with fine plumage. I saw eight more behind the lodge, some sitting on posts, but no greyhens. The time being 11.30, probably they had just finished sparring at the lek. Next I walked to the plantation, mainly of Scots fir, which has not been thinned. I saw a blackcock, but only skirted the wood, which would need most of a day to explore thoroughly.

I descended to the burn, flushing a snipe in a bog and seeing a frog. I struck a 'sheep's roadie' (path) among grass. Junipers stretch for several hundred yards, and mixed grass and heather patches cover most of the hill except a rocky part around the summit. Amongst the junipers and grass I saw many skylarks and meadow pipits, and 17 pairs of grouse from Morven Lodge to the shoulder west of the summit. Wheatears abounded as far up as the first shoulder, many peewit pairs rose, and curlews continually flew over, wailing and uttering bubbling calls. Peewits have not started laying here yet.

At the top of the shoulder I had lunch above a big snowdrift, and passed more drifts further up. The summit has many boulders and a cairn at 2860 feet. Mr Seton Gordon told me that if I climbed Morven I might see ptarmigan at the top. Not having seen any, I determined to try to find one before stopping to look at the view. A moment after, when I had gone ten yards down the north side, a beautiful cock ptarmigan with fine crimson comb suddenly rose from my feet and ran down the hill a short distance. When I followed, it ran further, and then flew to alight at 2500 feet.

Returning to the cairn, I looked at the view, simply magnificent. Loch Muick lay in a hollow, and I saw Lochnagar, the Cairngorms, and lower Deeside, with Loch Davan and Loch Kinord burning like golden bars and Mount Keen sharply set against a slightly hazy sky. Away towards Loch Builg a big heather fire burned. A spotless snow blanket covered the rounded top of Ben Macdui, while through the telescope I saw the big black cairn standing out sharply against the surrounding white. Ben Avon looked as though whitewash had been emptied over it.

I arrived at the lodge, seeing 15 blackcocks but again no greyhens. A curlew flew out of tall grass and circled, wailing incessantly. While cycling down to Lary I saw eight golden plover in pairs and 12 peewits. In Glen Gairn, hooded crows sat in birches and I saw a rookery in firs at Bridge of Gairn. After arriving at Ballater I read the chapters on The Curlew, The Golden Plover, The Black Grouse, The Ptarmigan and The Oystercatcher in Seton Gordon's *Hill Birds of Scotland*.

1944. 11 April. To meet Seton Gordon

I heard that Seton Gordon is staying at Crathie. My brother Stewart telephoned them, and I am going up to meet them at 4 pm tomorrow. Am I excited!

12 April. Meeting Seton Gordon

The weather was beautiful. I left on cycle at 3, and as it was only 3.30 at Balmoral I climbed Craig Gowan and Creag an Lurachain. Then I ran to meet Mr and Mrs Gordon coming out of Craig Gowan house. We shook hands and I told him I had been up the hills. Formalities over, we began to 'talk birds'. He said in the west Highlands there is a race between heron and raven as to which nests first, and I told him herons were nesting near Turriff on March 11. We walked to his aunt's house near the school at Crathie.

Then we set off with his collie Dara up the wood, seeing innumerable chaffinches. He said the Braemar, Ballater and Aboyne chaffinches have different songs, but on account of increasing deafness he cannot now hear birdsong. He hoped to find a woodcock nest, but there was not enough bracken. Two sparrow-hawks flew up and down like pigeons. We reached a moor where many curlews sang, and he confided the locations of eagle nests, which must be kept secret. I had supper with them and left at 9.30 for Ballater. At Coilacriech a woodcock was roding.

1944. 13 April. Out with Seton Gordon

Weather again was beautiful. I left Ballater at 9.30 and arrived just before 10. In the garden, SG had seen a crossbill in a fir and we watched house sparrows nest-building on the house. He got sandwiches ready and then we left on foot for an eagle nest, I wheeling my bike for a mile. Here we had a magnificent view of a cock capercaillie on a dead tree, and he said caper nested here last year. On the moor were many curlews and some grouse. A few peewits rose but had not started laying eggs yet, as those at Turriff have (nest with three eggs on 3 April). A few snipe flew from a bog and curlews sang along the whole moor. Some common gulls sailed over, and he said 5–6 pairs nested at Sandy Loch when last he visited, one of them on a rock in the loch. He saw only a few ptarmigan on Lochnagar in 1943, but hundreds when he was young.

AW and young Willie Hutcheon in Glen Derry, July 1944

In a fir wood we saw a sparrow-hawk and old nests of wood-pigeons, and at last reached the rocks, but alas the eyrie had broken down. The eagle may be using another eyrie, but a second one on the rock had also broken down. Now we went through ancient Scots firs and he pointed out a goosander's nest-hole in a dead fir, which gamekeepers had burned. He saw it occupied in the 1910s and was disappointed to see it burnt. A lizard sunned itself on a rock.

Crossing the moor again, we found a dead fox. Then we parted where I left my bike, for I intended to cycle up another glen to check an eyrie he had described. I cycled along the track and sped down a steep brae. Braking on gravel at a corner, I went head over heels past the handlebars and down a bank, skinning knees and elbows. The bike was intact, though slightly bent, but now I felt sore and stiff, so I cycled by the main road to Ballater. It has been the best day of my life.

15 April. An eagle eyrie with an early eaglet

Weather dull. Today I went to an eyrie SG told me about, many miles up Deeside to cycle and walk. Hiding my bicycle, I walked up a wood where a fine cock capercaillie stood at the top of a tree. The wood was silent, except for the sough of wind in the trees and the rush of the burn. Walking through tall heather, I often tripped on hidden stones and fell into holes full of water.

Among sparse trees I saw a huge bird sailing on motionless pinions above, like a large blanket driven before the wind, a handsome golden eagle. It disappeared behind the hill and next I spotted the old fir with the eyrie. While eating sandwiches, I noticed a pair of meadow pipits chasing.

I started to climb to the old fir. Slowly I walked along rocks, and then had a magnificent view, one I shall never forget in all my life, of a beautiful hen eagle. Craning her neck, she glared over the eyrie edge, stretched her wings and flapped heavily off. Soon over a distant hillside, she sailed and soared. Far from golden, she was pale yellowish brown. The earlier one was presumably the cock. The nest, a huge structure lined with fresh fir-shoots, stretched five feet deep by five feet wide. Higher up the hill, I looked with the telescope and saw a white downy chick.

Later I saw the remains of an eyrie on a rock. Then I climbed a steep gully with small rocks to reach a hilltop, where I heard a distant rumble of thunder to the south, while a drizzly shower came on. Separate pairs of grouse and meadow pipits abounded, even near the eyrie. Indeed, one cock grouse crowed loudly a few yards downhill from the eyrie tree. I saw more grouse than on any hill so far on Deeside. So much for the notion that eagles kill most of the grouse!

I guessed the time as 2 o'clock and for the next hour and a half searched vainly for another nest. Now I ate my cake and cheese sandwiches, drank water from the burn, walked through tall heather, and down for miles to my bicycle. On the Dee shingle stood 25 common gulls. Cycling back I saw stock doves in a birch-wood and two sparrow-hawks gliding.

1944. 5 July. To see the eaglet

Dad and I cycled to see how the eagles were doing since my visit on 15 April. As I came under the tree, I heard scraping above. Next moment a mass of droppings, bones, other refuse and dead heather flopped over the eyrie edge to splash on a rock below, missing my face by inches. Now an eaglet craned its neck over the edge. It looked huge and almost black, save for a few white feathers on neck and wings, and white on the base of its tail. It shuffled on its feet. As it flapped, its wings struck a branch above. After a few more shuffles, it flew at least ¼ mile out of sight.

On the way down the glen I spotted a white fleck on the steep hill far above. The telescope swung into action and revealed the eaglet sitting on a boulder below a cliff, flapping its wings. As we waited, a dark shape crossed the sky, the hen returning. I noticed the cock standing like a statue at the cliff-top, looking down to the eaglet. The hen stopped circling, and we watched her close her wings and dive to the cliff with the wind whistling through her pinions.

8 July. With Mr Hutcheon and son Willie to Ben Macdui

It was a perfect morning at Luibeg, sunny and warm. The sun dried the soaked firs, giving off a lovely smell. Chaffinches ran on the wet grass and wood pigeons flew in the firs. At the footbridge well up Glen Derry we saw several common gulls, and two stood on stunted firs, crying loudly. Snow lay in specks on Carn Crom and a small drift by the Lochan Uaine waterfall. At the entrance to Coire Etchachan we heard bleating from scores of calves with hinds. Sandpipers had been numerous all the way up the glen, but we saw none after the entrance to the corrie.

A stiff climb followed up the corrie, where an eagle sailed. We had a cup of tea at Loch Etchachan and then climbed, taking a drink at a snow-covered burn. The walls of the ruined OS bothy provided shelter for lunch, and we looked at an immense snow wreath to the north. Next we strolled to the top of Ben Macdui for a grand view of Cairn Toul and Braeriach, the latter splashed with snow, but could not see distant hills because of haze. Then we descended to the March Burn, which had a snow drift, and at Coire Mor saw the wreckage of a plane and a memorial cairn.

Skirting Coire Mor, we reached Coire Clach nan Taillear with big drifts. Mr Hutcheon and I glissaded for a hundred yards down one wreath. Then we all walked to the saddle towards Carn a' Mhaim, seeing a pair of ptarmigan which ran off croaking loudly, so evidently they had young. A quick descent to Dee followed, and then a five-mile walk to Luibeg. Tired young Willie had to be given a 'backie' on his father's back for a hundred yards. At Luibeg, plates of steaming tattie soup, fish and potatoes awaited us, and then we splashed in the burn and went to bed at 9 pm.

9 July. At Luibeg

Today was sunny and warm. Mr Hutcheon went to Cairn Toul and I stayed to give company to the tired young Willie, although I would have liked to climb. Miss George told me she saw two young cuckoos sitting on the deer fence beside the house this summer, and a greyhen's egg in Derry wood last week, evidently addled. A robin pair nested at the cottage this year. Mr Beattie found a dead young eagle in the wood a year or two ago, and he kept the wing, some feathers of which he gave us. Two pairs of oystercatchers are on the grassy flat. Willie and I fished vainly with bent pins in the forenoon, and in the afternoon I searched Derry wood, seeing a blackbird's nest in a spruce and several robins. After Mr Hutcheon arrived from Cairn Toul for tea, I cycled to Linn of Dee with him. We saw several curlews and pairs of golden plover in Glen Lui.

10 July. To Ballater

Beautiful and sunny. We cycled back to Ballater, stopping at Invercauld to see a man land a big fish.

11 July. Craig Coillich

Again sunny. In the forenoon I climbed Craig Coillich, now devoid of trees except at the foot, where the birches and tall bracken held many mistle and song thrushes, chaffinches and willow warblers. All the way to the top at 1300 feet, the brushwood left from the felling was alive with wrens and dunnocks, and an occasional robin and blackbird. I had a good view at the top. In the afternoon I cycled away up Glen Muick to fish, and watched a heron being chased by three crows and two rooks. It flew at treetop height, jerking and swerving to avoid its loud-voiced sable pursuers. They left the heron a moment later, but no sooner had that excellent fisherman reached the river, when a jackdaw flew from a tree to chase off the great clumsy bird.

12 July. Lochnagar

Weather beautiful. Dad and I cycled up the west side of Glen Muick with the moor on our left and a fir wood on our right. On the moor we saw a few peewits, snipe and many curlews. One curlew pair circled, and then flew low, uttering a human-like 'ha-ha-ha-ha' and a wild shriek of alarm, so probably had young. After hiding bicycles at Allt-na-giubhsaich we walked up the path and had lunch at a stone butt. Before the steep part, I found a cold spring near the path. Refreshed, we soon reached the top of the Ladder slope at 3500 feet, where I spotted the sea at Montrose. Soon we reached the plateau, with a pleasant walk on turf to a cairn at Cac Carn Mor.

We stopped to look down the Black Spout and saw many swifts, some of them screaming, flying around the cliffs and summit rocks. The fine day had attracted 16 walkers, and Dad and I spent an hour enjoying a splendid view. The Caithness hills, Ben Nevis and the Fife Lomonds rose clear, and through a telescope I saw the flag on Invercauld hotel at Ballater. A common gull flew over. Dad sprained a wrist while walking down the Ladder and I had a puncture down the glen, but we took these in our stride. We had had a grand day on the hill.

In my diary for 12 September I wrote: 'My article about Swallows attacking a Kestrel was published in The Banffshire Journal today. I also received a letter from George Waterston, Secretary of the S.O.C., who is coming up to investigate Rooks and Wood Pigeons'. Seeing a solicitor's office at my address, with 'Stewart & Watson' on the window, George went in one late afternoon. A receptionist ushered him to my father Adam Watson, then 48 years old and sole solicitor. George said Mr Alexander had suggested he see Adam Watson. My father said "It's not me you want to see, it's my son Adam. He's the bird watcher. He's still at school, but please have a coffee and he'll be home soon". Shortly I came and was delighted to meet George Waterston, a name I knew well from ornithological publications. Afterwards George recalled his surprise when I appeared in shorts, an old jacket, and no tie. George later told Mr Alexander, who had assumed from my detailed letters and survey reports that I was an adult. George arranged to come next Saturday morning, 23 September, for a day.

Long ere the appointed time, I sat in feverish excitement at a window, gazing at the corner where his car would appear. When it did, I ran down to meet him. My diary runs: 'Mr Waterston arrived at 10 am and we set out in his car for Forglen'. Later we explored Delgaty lake and then 'We struck up the hill to the east of the lake and flushed a beautiful capercaillie cock with a glinting blue neck at the edge of a plantation, where there were two mistle thrushes and a few wood-pigeons and hoodies. Mr Waterston had tea with us and kindly gave me two little books to read..'

Chapter 3. 1945

Saturday 3 February, after a very cold snowy January. Newburgh

Mr Waterston and I set off at 12 noon, via Fyvie. We went into Fyvie Wood to see Main the keeper. He said the pigeons had taken their flight, as at Turriff and Huntly, and only a very few remained. All the pigeons flew away whenever the last big storm commenced, but this time they stayed for several days after the first snow, because they had plenty of turnip-tops and not so much snow as the last severe winter, so the turnips were not wholly covered by snow at first. Next we went on the road again, and saw some very interesting birds ¼ mile south of Fyvie. At a stack-yard were 4 pigeons and a couple of magpies. The magpies sat on a rick each and were real beauties and very near us. A fine kestrel hovered over us into a birch wood. We noticed a rookery at Meldrum House.

There now followed a run over a terrible road – the only vehicle before us had been a tractor clearing the road. Near Pitmedden at 1 pm were 17 pigeons at stacks, 22 more in some nearby beech trees, and three flew out of an old thorny hedge. There was a flock of some 50 to 60 rooks on stacks and 10 on dung-heaps. The rook certainly pulls stacks to bits to get at the corn (oats) – straw lies thick around the bottom of each rick, but this happens only when the rick is loose and badly built. Sixteen pigeons flew over, one was on a stack, two flew over, 25 rooks were on a corn-heap and 5 on a stack, while 10 flew out of a quarry probably for grit and then 100 on stacks.

This paragraph was not in my diary but I recall the events as if yesterday. At Fontainebleu we crossed to the road for Newburgh, and shortly afterwards a striking scene appeared ahead..As the car breasted a summit on the road, suddenly we saw bright green fields that held little snow, leading to Newburgh with its church tower. Beyond, the Ythan mudflats and tidal river shone in the sunshine, with a huge yellow sand dune on the far side and then the great expanse of the blue North Sea. The sight caught my excitement and wonder. The place seemed so different from anywhere else on the coast. Ever since, as I breast that summit the view jumps to my attention. As I type this, I see the panorama and colours in my imagination, so vividly that I feel I am there again.

We arrived at Newburgh and went to see Dr Edgar Smith at Culterty. He showed us a white-breasted barn owl, which he had found dead, and which was extremely thin. (it had probably died of starvation). Smith thought it was a snowy owl! Dugald McIntyre mentions that the barn owl is the least hardy of British owls.

Then Smith showed us round his "zoo". This is a large tract of ground, with three small lakes, dotted with islands. Two lakes are salt water, one of fresh. The salt-water lakes change their water every day by the tides. Most of the lakes are frozen. There are dozens of nesting-boxes on the islands and also many trees and collections of brushwood between the lakes. The furthest corner is a plantation.

On the lawn were a pair of Tasmanian geese, which had made their nest (this is their summer). Their feet are something like a coot's. On the fresh-water lake was an exciting collection of various ducks, all very tame, and nearly all able to fly about at will. There were mallard, beautiful wigeon with clear whistles, teal, pochard, a beautiful drake shoveler, ruddy shelducks, a beautiful pintail, tufted ducks and many foreign species.

He gave Mr Waterston a newly dead robin for David Lack (robin expert at Oxford). A crane in the garden had flown to the Duthie Park in Aberdeen from Helsinki Zoo. It sleeps out in the middle of the pond with its head under its wing in the recent howling blizzards. It is very tame, has an unearthly cry, huge wings, and very long, dark legs.

On the salty lake were many geese – greylag, bean, pink-footed, Canada geese, barnacles and brents. I noted the main difference between the dark-breasted brent and the Canada goose -- the Canada has a large white spot near its beak. Several barnacles planed down to the ice, and reached it so quickly that their legs fairly twinkled along the ice trying to stop themselves. There were also many foreign geese here and waterhens. Smith said he saw a great grey shrike in the hedge last year.

Then at 2.10 pm we went along to Bouck's house. Bouck is a wonderful man – a typical old naturalist. He has records of all the birds he has shot for 60 years and he shoots every day..

He also has, in this cosy little room, several magnificent paintings of varieties of woodcock. One painting is unique. It shows the only case of albinism and melanism together in one woodcock. Bouck says he has shot woodcock in all colours – buff, creamy, rufous, dark brown, and a mixed orange-white.

Bouck said they sometimes get little auks up the estuary, and several men took 200 dozen seagulls' eggs off the Bullers of Buchan last summer. About geese, he said they would always go inland promptly whenever there was young corn.

He once saw a glossy ibis on a marsh at Newburgh, and soon someone shot it. A man came to the door and said "Whit's this bird?" Bouck replied"It's a glossy ibis". "Oh! I thocht it wis a cross atween a craw and a curlew". Bouck "What are you going to do with it?" "Bung't awa". Bouck "I'll give you two and sixpence for it". So the man pocketed the "half croon" and Bouck had the ibis.

Bouck said he knew of a pochard 27 years old. He knew of a partridge breeding in its seventh year though they are supposed to be of no use after three years. The seven year-old partridge was a white male, easily recognised. Though pretty tame, it was shot one day.

Now at 4.20 pm we had to go, so we said goodbye and we would be back soon after the thaw. We decided to go home by a better road via Aberdeen, Inverurie and Oldmeldrum. Soon we reached Aberdeen, and noticed small icebergs on the Don. Near Hatton at 6.20 pm, I saw my greatest gathering of rooks before they go to roost. Several fields were literally black with them and they rose in dense clouds to fly to the wood. There were thousands and thousands of them. We arrived at Turriff in time for tea and then I saw Mr Waterston off.

12 July. Ben Avon

Sunny, but cloudy in the afternoon. After breakfast in Ballater, Dad drove with Stewart and me to Corndavon Lodge and reached the ruined Lochbuilg Lodge at 10.20. Here a peewit pair flapped anxiously, obviously with chicks. We struck up Carn Dearg and reached a path that led us to 2800 feet, where we stopped to have lunch beside a cold burn rushing in cascades. The only sound was the piping of a golden plover among peat hags. At 3000 feet we saw a pair of golden plovers with young, and had fine close views, the cock beautiful with his black and white front.

Climbing to the tops of the two tors at Stuc Gharbh Mhor, we looked across to a little corrie with huge snow wreaths, and saw many hinds and calves on the grass. From the tor of Clach Choutsaich we walked west to the summit, three hours from the loch. Meadow pipits had been numerous all the way from Corndavon to the topmost rock, where I spotted a fledged chick with down on its head. From the cairn on the top we had a very fine view beyond the Moray Firth, and also Ben Rinnes, Bennachie, Braemar village, and wild Slochd Mor and the corries of Beinn a' Bhuird with snow patches.

About 100 swifts raced about the tors. The number around the high hills seems to depend on weather. For instance, in July 1944 I climbed Lochnagar twice. On a fine day I saw over 200, but on a cold misty drizzly day only three. Soon we descended, at 2700 feet seeing four pairs of golden plovers with young, four grouse pairs without young and a hen grouse with three fledged young.

Reaching Loch Builg two hours after leaving the top, we drove off, but the car stuck in a short peaty stretch. The more we tried, the deeper it sank, until its axle sat on the road. While Stewart walked to the lodge for help, I waded at Loch Builg's sandy beach. When I returned, the gamekeeper had just arrived with Stewart. Further efforts to extricate our car failed, so we packed into his small car and so to Ballater.

He has been 10 years at Corndavon. Snow blocked the road for 13 weeks in 1939. He thought this was bad until 1940 when snow cut them off for 20 weeks from the end of December till the middle of May. This year, the Gab (Beginning) o May snowstorm played havoc with all nesting birds, and he sees very few young grouse.

17 July. With James Beattie at Luibeg

It was warm and sunny as Mr Beattie had foretold. After breakfast, Stewart and I walked up Glen Luibeg, where I watched six redstarts in old firs, a lovely hen merlin gliding, and sandpipers common along the burn. Later we fished Derry Burn and I had 13 trout, some of a fair size. In the afternoon I searched Luibeg wood, finding four redstarts. In the evening, Stewart and Mr Beattie had a shooting competition, in which Beattie proved very accurate despite his age. Shots from his .303 rifle echoed loudly from hill to hill.

Mr Beattie says there are a few capercaillie and blackgame up Derry wood, and on the moor "files a puckle o faaps (whiles a few curlews) an golden plover, bit naething like as mony golden plover as Strathdon or Glen Livet" (pronounced Leevit). A great character, when drinking his tea he pours some into the saucer and puts it to his lips, making a noise like a suction-dredger at work! He tears savagely at buns, and eats his cement-like hard porridge with a gloomy air. Dr Grieve, an Aberdeen medical doctor and photographer, is on holiday with his family in a caravan at the Black Brig. When Dr Grieve said he had seen a golden eagle, Beattie replied, "Ach man, ye dinna ken the first damned thing aboot birds. There's nae sik thing as a *golden* eagle here, they're aa *black* eagles. I'll bet ye jist saw a bloody craa". Several hikers today called at the house asking for boiling water and food. At big prices they got some of Beattie's old loaf bread that he keeps for feeding the hens!

18 July. Carn Crom

Sunny and warm again. Stewart and I fished Derry Burn in the forenoon. In the afternoon I went to Carn Crom to visit the small cliffs and look into Glen Derry. I found a live two-inch mortar and several warheads. I noticed a large number of very young fir seedlings but suppose the deer will eat them soon. Mr Beattie does not need to prune the rose in front of the house. The deer do it for him, up to five feet, and above that the bush bulges out. I reported the mortar to Mr Beattie who said he would let the army know.

19 July. At Luibeg

At 10 am heavy rain started and increased to a downpour. Suddenly, a brilliant flash of lightning split the gloom, followed a few seconds later by thunder. Mr Beattie jumped as if struck by the lightning and ran to the stable, worried and mumbling about Donald the horse, who stood shivering very near the deer fence. After another flash and rumble, Donald started jumping up and down in fear. Beattie came out of the stable with a lasso and a piece of bread, and deftly threw the lasso over Donald's neck in cowboy fashion before leading him out at the gate and into the stable. Then Beattie returned to the house as the storm drew nearer. Two flashes came together, followed instantaneously by a terrific crash of thunder which lasted a long time. The cat jumped about in the kitchen and Miss George said "You're the only een that canna keep quait", to which Beattie said "It'll seen keep quait fan it's pit ootside."

Then two people passed the window in torrential rain. "Twa fowk fae Aviemore nae doot", said Beattie, "fit'll they be needin?" But the two were Dad and Mr Tucker, who had come in Dad's car to Derry Lodge. Mr Beattie warned them that the burn at the ford below Clais Fhearnaig would soon be too high for the car to cross, so after a quick lunch we set off. The colour of strong tea, the Luibeg Burn roared down, rushing with great force against the bridge props and surrounding both ends of the footbridge. We just managed to cross the burn below Clais Fhearnaig by rushing at speed through it. On ordinary days the burn runs underneath the stones on the road, but today roared in a torrent 1–2 feet above.

26 July. With Bernard W. Tucker to Cairn Toul

A sunny morning. After breakfast, Mr Tucker and I left by cycle for Cairn Toul, seeing many redpolls in the birches. Crossing the Canadian Brig at the lumber camp, now used also by mules and light artillery troops, we headed up Glen Lui. I spotted an eagle sailing and we got lovely views of it through binoculars, a bird very light in colour. At Luibeg we left our bikes. When we told Miss George we would search the Lui wood tomorrow, she said we should stay tonight at Luibeg to save going to Braemar and back, but Mr Tucker could not join me, because as editor he has to correct proofs of the August *British Birds*.

I asked Mr Beattie what today's weather would be like, to which he replied "ye wid be aa richt", without giving detail. We cycled up the path and hid bikes in heather near the footbridge over Luibeg Burn. The path round Carn a' Mhaim keeps fairly level at 2000 feet before dipping to Glen Dee with a grand view of Glen Geusachan. A short shower came on and I spotted a couple of eagles, an old and a young bird. A big snow wreath remained on Monadh Mor despite a warm spring and summer. We waded across Dee below Corrour Bothy, where we had a magnificent view of the great flanks of Ben Macdui, the shapely cone of Cairn Toul with its cairn perched on the edge of a hanging corrie, and the massive cliffs of the Devil's Point. Deep snow filled a gully on Coire Clach nan Taillear of Ben Macdui and two tattered patches lay in Coire Bhrochain.

After ascending a path up Coire Odhar beside a leaping burn, we ate our lunch half way up. A heavy shower came on but soon ceased, although mist stayed on Ben Macdui. After a short steep climb we reached the top of the corrie, next walked up the grassy slope of the Buidheanach, and then over boulders to a cairn above Coire an t-Saighdeir. A ptarmigan with four tiny downy chicks flapped anxiously when two chicks ran towards the cliff. Mist now swept in, and continuous rain fell. A cold wind bit one's cheek, so I wrapped a woollen scarf round my head while we dipped down past the Slichit.

The final route from the Slichit rose over boulders. With sudden gusts of wind tearing at times, we had to be very careful to avoid slipping. When at last we reached the summit cairn, our hands felt numb with grasping wet boulders and we could not see more than ten yards. Well, I now stood at the top of Cairn Toul (4241 feet), but would have rather had a clearer day for my first visit. We stayed only a minute. A man arrived with no waterproof and a shirt soaking, so I think he would not have enjoyed his round to Braeriach and away back to Glen Feshie.

Now we began to descend carefully on wet boulders to the Slichit. For a moment we saw Sgor an Lochain Uaine through a gap in swirling mist that rushed down into Coire an t-Saighdeir. We hurried down the Buidheanach in increasing wind and torrential rain. Soon the water squelched in our boots and we stopped to take them off. I took a boot off, let water run out, and rinsed the stocking, but it would hardly fit into the boot again, so I did not take off the other boot. While having a short rest we heard a dotterel and I noticed a pair close, running up the slope.

We descended Coire Odhar fairly quickly, seeing a few young frogs, and soon arrived at Corrour Bothy where we took tea inside, out of the rain. The one-room bothy has a large open fireplace and is sturdily built, but falling to pieces. Holes in the metal roof are plugged with paper, and a mass of sods covers one end. Until a few years ago there used to be a nice armchair and wooden cupboard, but hikers broke these up for firewood, although if they had troubled they could have found firewood in the roots of fir trees in the peat.

Now we waded Dee less carefully than on the way up, and walked the path to the shoulder of Carn a' Mhaim where we saw a hen grouse with ten flying young. Here we looked back to wild Braeriach and the Lairig Ghru. Mist hung about the Devil's Point, giving it a gloomy look, while in contrast the hills to the south and east were clear. After a long walk round the seemingly interminable shoulder we reached our bikes near the first firs. Mr Tucker said he heard a probable crested tit here last year but got a very poor view, so was not at all certain. Now we had a bumpy ride on our bikes for a mile and a half. On reaching Luibeg at 6.30 we separated, Mr Tucker to go to Braemar and I to stay at Luibeg.

In the house my wet socks soon steamed before a roaring fire while I tucked into hot thick Scotch broth, fish and potatoes, and endless cups of tea with cake and biscuits. I finished at 7.30, and for the rest of the evening sat in front of the fire to dry my trouser legs. Mr Beattie used no paraffin light, the fire being enough. Miss George and I sat in arm chairs at either side of the fire, and Mr Beattie always sat on a wooden chair by a table inside the kitchen door. There he chewed tobacco, occasionally took snuff, and from time to time interrupted the talk of Miss George and me by saying "Aye, min" (man), and then spitting with unerring accuracy for three yards right across the room into the fire, which would sizzle each time. I got into bed at 9.30 pm and slept like a log at once.

27 July. Glen Derry and Glen Lui

I rose at 7.30 after a refreshing sleep. In clear spells I watched birds among firs near Luibeg, seeing many tree creepers, and some crossbills and redstarts. At about 11 the rain stopped and I walked up Glen Derry. Two capercaillies crashed through the trees. A thick drizzle came on and Toman Dearg gave a wild view to a Beinn Mheadhoin capped with driving mist.

At Luibeg they waited excitedly to hear election news from Mr Morgan the post, who arrived on his motor bike from Inverey. "Fa's in? To this he replied, "Churchill", but then added, "Na, though, it's Attlee," so I did not know till I met Mr Tucker near the Black Bridge. He said Churchill has about 190 MPs, while Labour has roughly twice as many, more than all others put together. Attlee is going to Potsdam with Bevin as Foreign Minister.

In Glen Lui we took our tea near the twisted old fir illustrated in the frontispiece of Seton Gordon's book *A Highland Year*. Then we crossed the Black Brig and searched the wood, seeing a roe deer. We left the brig at about 6 and had a pleasant run down to Braemar in ¾ of an hour. Later I walked to Mayfield and had a long talk with Mr Tucker, mostly about eagles. I got an interesting letter from Seton Gordon and saw 300 jackdaws in larch trees.

18 August. To Luibeg

Mr Hutcheon took me by car from Turriff and Mr Spence from Forgue, while Mr and Mrs Sheriffs from Turriff came in their car. At Braemar, the Sheriffs' bikes were waiting, and Mr Hutcheon and I cycled up to Inverey on them while Spence drove Mr Hutcheon's car. It was delightful cycling in the cool evening and the hills looked magnificent, especially Beinn a' Bhuird with creamy clouds resting on its summit. I noticed that Beinn Bhrotain still carried a large wreath in its south corrie, which had not decreased much since the end of July.

From Inverey, Mr Hutcheon drove Spence and me to Derry Lodge, where we put the car in a shed. After supper at Luibeg, Mr Beattie showed us round the lodge. Evidently the Cairngorm Club have first option if it is to be sold. We strolled up the Lairig, and, with a frosty touch in the air, it was delightful walking through the wood. Beinn Bhrotain looked imposing, black as night against a bright orange-red sky, and somewhere amongst the firs, an owl hooted twice. It was dark when we reached Luibeg, and after a long crack with Beattie, we went to bed after 11 pm.

19 August. Loch Avon and Ben Macdui

Mist was low in the morning, with showers, but beautiful later. After rising at Luibeg at 7.30 am, Mr Hutcheon, Mr Spence and I went to the burn to wash and then took our breakfast, having already made sandwiches for the climb and found a stout stick each. Leaving in high spirits at 9, we met Mary Farquharson of Braemar with three others, making for Braeriach, and then we walked up Glen Derry. A kestrel flew out of the wood with a flock of crows, and many crossbills fed in the treetops and dropped cones to the ground. As we crossed the footbridge two miles up, mist covered the top of the cliff on Beinn Mheadhoin and lay lower on Derry Cairngorm, so we began to wonder if we would reach Ben Macdui. About a mile further up, some gnarled firs grow on the stony slopes to the east. Here many mistle thrushes and ring ouzels mobbed a hen merlin, and I heard the sharp notes of a redstart amongst the babel of voices. Finally the merlin stooped at a mistle thrush, but, missing, flew up to a dead tree and ignored the mobbers.

In upper Glen Derry one seems to be keeping fairly level, but a glance at an altimeter at the head of the glen showed we had come up 700 feet already. Here the path forks, one over the Lairig an Laoigh and the other turning left into Coire Etchachan. A hundred hinds and calves grazed on Derry Cairngorm and 50 stags up Glas Allt Mor. The path does not climb much in the corrie at first, but then rises steep to the top, where one arrives suddenly at Loch Etchachan.

Mr Hutcheon and I quickly climbed to here, but Mr Spence, on account of his weight, had fallen behind and we waited ¼ hour for him. Meanwhile I searched for blaeberries, but the crop was pretty poor. Twenty ptarmigan flew over and the mist began to rise to the south, showing the sun for a while, but soon it swept along the loch again. At last Spence came at 11.30 and then we headed north. A pair of ptarmigan flew over and then we came on a path going steeply down the hill. At noon the mist suddenly cleared below us, to show a magnificent view of Loch Avon in a deep trench between Cairn Gorm and Beinn Mheadhoin. The loch's edges had a greenish colour, merging into blue-black in the centre. I had a great view of a ptarmigan as it sped on white wings above the water over to Cairn Gorm.

As we reached the Shelter Stone, the mist cleared. The blaeberry crop was amazing, the bushes laden with big succulent berries which we feasted on. The Shelter Stone has a small entrance, through which one stoops. The interior is dark as night, and stones and heather plug all holes. A cover slips over the entrance to keep out snow. A visitors' book lies at the entrance, rolled in waterproofs. We entered our names, and one also writes where one has been and is going.

After lunch, we ascended the course of the Feith Buidhe until it falls over the rocks, where we waited some time for Mr Spence. After traversing the slabs, on which the water runs in thin sheets, our route lay south-south-west over a maze of head-springs, clear cold pools and stony hollows where one could see that snow had lain recently, by means of the dark-coloured moss growing everywhere. The huge wreath to the north-east of the summit had completely gone, as had all the other drifts in these pockets, save one mere lump of snow lingering between Garbh Uisge Beag and Garbh Uisge Mor. Only a foot and a half long, a foot high, a foot broad and hard as a rock, one could not expect it to last a week in such fine weather. I flushed a pair of dotterel at one of these clear pools and they flew a short distance, uttering a liquid sweet note.

After a short climb we walked to the North Top and then over gravelly ground to the summit of Ben Macdui, which we reached at 2.45 as a thick bank of creamy mist came in from the north. The view was superb. Braeriach and Cairn Toul seemed close, and Ben Lawers, Stobinian and Ben Nevis stood out clearly. Sunshine bathed Aviemore and a train moved through the Spey woods. To the north and east, mist hid everything, but suddenly began to vanish and in a moment cleared again. In the Garbh Choire, snow still lingered in profusion.

It was delightfully warm on the summit but we had to be at Turriff tonight. We started back on excellent going over sandy stretches mingled with rocks, to the cliff-top where one suddenly looks down to Lochan Uaine far below. Here I heard a ring ouzel. A cool breeze ruffled the lochan and fanned the tattered rag of snow lying in a recess of the cliff, which slopes steeply into the loch at its western end. We took a short breather on a rocky outcrop and then quickly descended the Sron Riach on grass and short heather. The Lairig footpath lay about a mile beyond, and it cheered us to see the clump of gnarled old firs growing there. We saw Mr Spence half a mile behind, but Mr Hutcheon decided we should not wait.

At 5.15 pm we arrived at Luibeg, although Beattie thought we would be later. We came down in two hours and 15 minutes, pretty good going for we had waited ten minutes above Lochan Uaine for Spence. At the Luibeg burn we waded in with hot feet and splashed water in our faces. Mr Spence arrived half an hour after us, and by the time he came into the house, Mr Hutcheon and I were doing justice to a large dinner, with two helpings of thick broth, meat with Beattie's small but tasty potatoes, haggis, pudding and cups of tea. Miss George said a heron fished the burn for most of the day and I saw it as we left.

The car bumped down Glen Lui, where we picked up a hiker who had come through the Lairig from Aviemore. We ran fast down from Braemar to Ballater and the speedometer needle flicked round to 70 mph on the long straight stretch near Inver, while we did at least 60 mph most of the time. Reaching Ballater at 8, I flung my case into the car, saw Mum for a few moments, and then we tore on again, past Muir of Dinnet with the heather in beautiful bloom and the two lochs glittering like silver, and up a hill to the watershed. The scenery was lovely along the whole route, with scattered firs dotting the moors and long runs between tree-lined avenues. Soon we came to Strath Don and then Strath Bogie, where I saw big flocks of peewits, and down to Huntly which we reached in an hour from Ballater. Dusk had come when we dropped Mr Spence at Forgue. When we drove into Turriff quarter of an hour later, the new electric street lights had been switched on. As soon as we arrived I went into the house, ate my 'piece' (sandwiches) and then made for bed.

29 August

I received a letter from Miss George of Luibeg. She writes that very few people are going through just now, although one morning Mr Beattie found 'two young fellows up to the eyes in Donald's hay. They got a rude awakening, as you would expect, and had to quit immediately, this being done by forcible sayings on Mr Beattie's part!'

1 September. Pools of Dee

Today became unusually warm and sunny after a frost with ice on the puddles. On such a magnificent morning, Willie Hutcheon, Dad and I left our waterproofs and made rapid progress. I watched a kestrel hang motionless above Coire na Poite, and later an adult eagle pair sailing and one of them alighting on Carn a' Mhaim. Dropping on the path into Glen Dee, we came to Clach nan Taillear. It would not have given much shelter to the three tailors who died there in a snowstorm according to legend.

Above the rough narrow path, steep hills rise on either side. Near where Allt a' Choire Mhoir rushes over the path we got our first view of the Garbh Choire and the Dee falling over the precipice. The snow in Garbh Choire Mor had not decreased much since 19 August, but the lower ends of each wreath now looked grey with icy snow. The only other snow on the Dee side of the Cairngorms is a small wreath on Beinn Bhrotain, which will probably disappear in a week.

Here the path ascends to the Pools of Dee. We had to cross big boulders and then the first pool lay before us, a beautiful sight. Although shrunk by dry weather, it was bigger and deeper than I expected, and many small trout swam in the clear water or jumped at flies on the surface. After lunching there we walked back, reaching Luibeg at 6 after a fine long day and an 18-mile walk.

Chapter 4. 1946

15 April. To an eagle eyrie

Very warm and sunny for our climb to the eagle rock. When the nest held young last year, you could see them from below, but eggs are a different matter. I tried from the north at an almost perpendicular face covered with spiky wood rush and heather. Leaving my binoculars at the foot, I climbed to a broad ledge. There was no escape above, so I descended. Then I climbed up a gully running up the centre, but this petered out into loose boulders, so I had to go back. Finally I tried from the south. I reckoned I would be able to peer over, but there was a very tricky bit on the way. This was a rock slanting on to a loose crag, and one had to pass by getting one's tackets sideways on to the rock and tightening one's muscles. By gripping a birch sapling by one hand, I was able to peer down past the overhang. The nest was empty and flattened right below. I drew back at once, and, on the way back, loosened a large boulder which hindered easy passage along the rock. It shot off, and split like a thunderclap on the top of the crags into scores of pieces, one of which reached the road below. It was then that an adult eagle fluttered close over the crags above me and barked loudly once, before sailing off. Obviously she had another nest with eggs somewhere near.

18 April. Ben Macdui

At Ballater last night I phoned James Anton. A member of the Scottish Mountaineering Club and Scottish Ornithologists' Club, he is at Colqhonnie Hotel, owned by a friend of his. We arranged to come for him today, cold after a heavy morning frost, and mainly cloudy with sunny periods. Dad and I left Ballater at 9 to pick up James and his brother in law Captain Bradbury. James saw three goosander pairs on Don yesterday and nest scrapes of golden plover on Morven.

After visiting an eyrie where we saw a hen eagle sitting, we drove to Derry Lodge, to find the gate at the plantation locked. James lifted the gate off its hinges, but after driving through we could not get it back again. After we tried vainly for 20 minutes, I walked to Luibeg and got keys from Mr Beattie. On the way I noticed Beinn Mheadhoin looking lovely with fresh snow. We put the gate back on its hinges, and made a late start at 1 pm. When I returned the keys, Mr Beattie said "Ye'll nivver win ti Ben Macdui the day, it's ower black", pointing to the sky with his pipe.

However, in an hour we reached the foot of Sron Riach, where we lunched. Then we climbed up Sron Riach, with fine wild views across to Cairn Toul. Frequent hailstorms swept in from the north, and though most snow below 3000 feet had melted, above 3250 feet we came into dry snow, much of it blown into deep drifts and cornices. Bradbury had been leading, with me 100 yards behind him, but at 3000 feet I got a second wind and went well ahead at 3500 feet.

This spot gave a magnificent view of Lochan Uaine below. Snow filled the corrie and an avalanche had fallen from a bare rock face to the north. Snow had piled 25 feet deep at one end of the loch, and ice covered the inner part of the loch except where the burn runs out. The ice had previously broken into floes, which had partly frozen together again. The white ice sheets against the dark blue-green water made a fine contrast. Now we climbed to the plateau, where fresh snow lay several inches deep with many drifts. On a slope beside the summit, heavy snow fell and clouds of drift up to 12 feet high flew along the frozen hard surface of the old snow. Ice and frozen fog crystals covered the cairn, and now a thin mist came down as snow flakes whirled past on a bitterly cold wind. We walked over to the North Top, and suddenly out of the mist and snowflakes came a man and woman. Bradbury greeted the man, "Livingstone, I presume". Not a flicker of a smile crossed the man's gloomy countenance. Coming from the Shelter Stone, they now headed for Corrour Bothy.

Shortly the mist cleared off all the hills and we had fine views of Cairn Gorm and Beinn Mheadhoin. An immense snow wreath lay south-east of the North Top, where we took some photographs and changed a film. Meanwhile, ominous clouds had piled to the north-west, so we hurried through heavy ground drift to the top above Coire Sputan Dearg to have an exhilarating look down the cliff to the corrie far below. Now we saw hills very far off, Ben Alder, Binnein Mor and Ben Lawers, but clouds to the north-west pressed closer. While we had a cup of tea at 3500 feet the storm broke, and heavy hail and snowflakes swept along, adding to the huge cornices on Coire an Lochain Uaine hanging many feet over the cliff edge. We arrived at Luibeg at 7 pm after two and a half hours from the summit.

Surprised to hear that we reached the top, Mr Beattie ushered us to the kitchen, where Miss George gave us refreshing cups of hot tea and a thick 'piece' of bread and jam. She said they had no showers at Luibeg. On the way down, I counted 240 stags between Luibeg and the Black Bridge. At 8.30 we arrived at Ballater, where we had a fine meal with plenty of squash to drink. I gave James a loan of James Fisher's *Watching Birds* to read. Dad left with them at 9.30 for Strath Don, and Dad returned with several of James's bird books for me to read.

9 July. On Braeriach and Cairn Toul

Today was very warm and sunny, with a west wind and some clouds. Dad and I motored to Derry Lodge after collecting a key for the Lui gate at the estate office, where I saw a wood warbler in a beech tree. We left Luibeg at 11.30 am, seeing three redstarts in old firs up Glen Luibeg, where Beattie bawled at his dogs to stop them worrying a young roe they had caught. In Glen Luibeg we saw wheatears and ring ouzels perching on trees, and ring ouzels were common at the last trees.

We came to Allt Clach nan Taillear at 2 pm and had lunch while looking at a snow patch in Coire Clach nan Taillear. At 2.30 we started climbing Braeriach below the Pools of Dee, a stiff pull into the corrie and steep zigzag path to the lip. On the way up we saw a ptarmigan with eight small downy young, which rolled and tumbled down steep rocks none the worse. Reaching the top at 4.10 pm we met four people, one a keen ornithologist. We could see past the Culbin Sands and Moray Firth to Caithness. Great views opened to the south and west, but we did not know the hills there. A thunderstorm raged about Kincardineshire, with mist low on the hills.

I scrambled down to see the young Dee going over the precipice and saw a dotterel beside the Wells of Dee. A blistering sun beat down. On the south top I flushed a ptarmigan with two flying young. Then I met Dad above the Garbh Choire Mor, where we looked down to huge snowfields and snow-filled gullies. A few snow patches lay in Coire an Lochain Uaine of Cairn Toul, on Ben Macdui plateau, in Garbh Choire Dhaidh and Coire Bhrochain. We then climbed over boulders to Cairn Toul. A ring ouzel and meadow pipits had fledged young at 4000 feet.

After reaching Cairn Toul at 6.15 we descended to Corrour in an hour, seeing some ptarmigan below the summit. Folk at the bothy gave us piping hot tea. We saw frogs and common sandpipers when we waded across Dee. A touch of frost lay in the glen, now still and quiet, with the hills silhouetted against an orange sky. At 9.30 after 21 miles we reached Luibeg where Miss George gave us tea. We started back at 10.40, reaching Ballater at midnight, after my best day on the hill yet.

29 July. To Luibeg

In the afternoon at I sorted food to take to Luibeg and left Ballater by cycle at 6 pm, facing a strong wind. It turned out a grand sunny evening. I reached Luibeg at 9.15, and after supper and a long talk with Mr Beattie I went to bed late. By then, clouds had appeared and thunder muttered up Glen Luibeg.

30 July. At Luibeg

Very wet and rainy. I fished the Luibeg and Derry Burns and caught 24 trout, one of good size in a deep pool by the cottage. In the evening I searched Luibeg wood and saw a cock and hen capercaillie and four redstarts. After a grand supper, we sat round the fire talking till 11 pm.

31 July. With James Beattie to Beinn Bhreac

A warm and sunny day dawned this morning, with the burns a beautiful mahogany colour after yesterday's rain. After a fine breakfast of hard porridge with a cup of cold milk, and fried trout with cups of tea, Mr Beattie and I climbed to 2750 feet on Beinn Bhreac to check the rain gauge at the end of the month. It held 8.3 inches of rain for July, compared with 5.89 at Luibeg. A cold wind blew at the summit of Beinn Bhreac. We walked over to the west top, where a grand view opened over Moine Bhealaidh. A herd of 300 stags grazed far out, and a hen ptarmigan with nine big young flew off this stony top. We sat there to eat our piece and afterwards Mr Beattie smoked his pipe. Then we walked down boggy ground to the fir wood on the east side of Glen Derry, and spread out to comb through it, seeing a great spotted woodpecker, a redstart and six blackcocks. It has many dead trees and only a very few young firs growing from blown stumps out of reach of red deer.

At Ben Macdui indicator, AW, James Anton and Captain Bradbury, 18 April 1946 (photo Adam Watson sen)

In the afternoon I fished Derry Burn at the pretty set of waterfalls, pools and small gorges towards the north end of the wood. I caught 30 trout, including one over ten inches and six over eight inches. At dinner time Miss George had cooked magnificent broth, followed by boiled salmon, boiled potatoes from Mr Beattie's plot at Derry, and fried trout and eggs. I have never tasted better oatcakes in my life. Then we had cups of hot dark tea and talked at the fireside until 10.30.

1 August. Derry Cairngorm

Today was sunny, but cloudy at times with a few showers. In the forenoon I climbed Derry Cairngorm, seeing a few ptarmigan on Little Cairngorm and seedling firs growing up to 2300 feet on Carn Crom. I had a grand view from Derry Cairngorm, with the Garbh Choire Mor snow patches prominent and snow lying north-east of Ben Macdui. After eating thick sandwiches I descended in an hour and a half, after two hours up.

In the afternoon I walked up Glen Derry to look for birds. After supper I cycled to Braemar, meeting Dr Grieve at his caravan by the Black Brig. In Inverey I spoke to Peterie Mackintosh the keeper, who saw two young eagles a few days ago. They have shot many goosanders and foxes, but he saw seven goosanders on Dee near Inverey recently. At Braemar I went to Mrs Grant's house next to Mayfield on Chapel Brae, and had cocoa, biscuits and fresh strawberries from Mrs Grant. She speaks Gaelic well.

11 August. Loch Avon and Ben Macdui

We were lucky to have the weather warm and sunny with a south-west wind, some clouds and one or two showers. Bernard Tucker, Dad and I set off at 10 am from Braemar for Derry Lodge in Dad's car, and I spotted an adult eagle flying low in Glen Lui. At Derry Lodge we left the car at 10.55, seeing many chaffinches feeding on seeds from hay spread for deer last winter. Just above the footbridge by the old Derry Dam we saw five lapwings, and at 12.45 lunched at Loch Etchachan.

AW, AW sen, Capt Bradbury in Snowy Corrie, 18 April 1946

Then we dropped to the Shelter Stone, where we ate blaeberries, signed a visitors' book and met Air Training Corps cadets from Glenmore Lodge. A stiff pull up Feith Buidhe followed and then round the rocks to Garbh Uisge Beag, where a snow wreath lay. BWT and I heard a snow bunting. Another wreath lay by Garbh Uisge Mor, where we saw a hen ptarmigan and six fully fledged young with traces of down, another hen with nine young, and four hinds at a sandy pool.

We reached the summit at 4 pm. The magnificent view included the Lammermuirs, Ben More Assynt and Ben Cruachan. When we moved to drink tea in the shade of the cairn, to my amazement a cock snow bunting flew off the cairn to alight on a stone six feet away. Dirty grey on the underparts, it had already begun to moult. I called to the others to see it. Doubtless crumbs dropped by walkers attracted it, and Bernard saw one at the cairn in summer 1944. Before leaving he picked up about 20 empty rusty tins to remove them from the hill. We had never seen anyone do this, a selfless act.

Leaving the top at 4.25 pm, we reached Luibeg at 6.40, seeing on the way a hen merlin on Sron Riach and an eagle. After a cup of tea at Beattie's we motored to Braemar, where I saw 40 swifts, many still screaming. I packed up, saying goodbye to the Tuckers and Mrs Grant. A frosty mist rose off the river on the way back, and Loch Davan reflected a full moon on its placid water.

30 December. A stormy day on Derry Cairngorm

After a cloudless sunny morning came a cold north-west wind with a hurricane high up. After breakfast Dad and I went by car from Ballater to Derry Lodge, seeing a few waterhens at Bridge of Gairn. Fresh snow had fallen since yesterday and Lochnagar looked very fine. Beinn a' Bhuird was pure white and snow plastered the tors on Ben Avon. A hen capercaillie flew across the road at Inverey, and at the foot of Lui the Canadian lumber huts have been demolished.

AW at Allt Phouple of Ben Avon, 21 July 1946 (photo Adam Watson sen)

AW with border terrier Duff at Cairn Gorm summit, 8 September 1946 (photo Adam Watson sen)

Thick ice covered parts of the road in Glen Lui. We drove to the lodge and walked to Luibeg, where 20 stags fed, one with a malformed horn and one with antlers devoid of points. Beattie and Miss George got a surprise on seeing us.

With two sticks we set off at 11.15. The sun shone warmly and we sweated to reach the rocky outcrop above the wood. Hard frozen ground along the ridge gave pleasant walking, but ice covered the rocks at the top of Carn Crom, where we had magnificent close-up views of four pure white ptarmigan. Big drifts had piled up at the col above Coire na Saobhaidh. We made rapid progress up to Little Cairngorm. The snow had been hard all the way but occasionally let a foot through. We had a cup of tea out of the strong wind and then held on to the final cone.

Driven by a severe gale, drifting snow tore along, covering trousers, coat and helmet white. Head-on against it, we toiled up the cone. I moved ahead of Dad and took a breather in a snowy hollow behind a boulder. Then I struggled up and on the last lap the hurricane threw me on the snow several times. I crawled on hands and knees along boulders, finding it hard to breathe in the choking drift. Suddenly a white shape rose like a big snowman, the summit cairn. For the last few yards I staggered up to my knees in soft snow. At the leeward side I kicked out a hollow in the snow and rested till Dad came. Beautiful yellowish fog crystals encrusted the cairn and boulders. The impressive view stretched to Beinn a' Bhuird pure white, Ben Macdui's cliffs thick with snow, and cloud on the rest of the high Cairngorms. Snow clouds raced over Beinn a' Ghlo, where a shaft of sunlight glittered on a river in Glen Tilt.

We hurried off the top, for we felt cold in the hurricane. As soon as we had gone 20 yards downhill the wind dropped to gale force. On the way down to Little Cairngorm I glissaded 50 feet in two places, great fun. Then we descended rapidly to Carn Crom, seeing fox tracks at 3100 feet, a grouse at 3000 feet and 12 white ptarmigan flying off. Hurrying black clouds came down to 3500 feet, a wild and beautiful scene. Below Carn Crom we saw three deer calves with eight hinds and 15 stags. Luibeg we reached at 3 pm, after two hours up, and less time on descent. In the wood, numerous coal tits fed in tall heather, and they and many tree creepers in the trees.

We had grand tea at Beattie's, walked to Derry Lodge, and bumped down the road. Thirty stags grazed at Luibeg and 70 on the armed services' former football pitch at Dalrossie in Glen Lui. A most enjoyable day, one of the best I have spent in the hills. I had slightly sore eyes at night, due to sun glittering on the snow.

31 December. Muir of Dinnet

A coating of snow lay down to 900 feet today, then sunny and warm, with snow clouds passing on a north-west wind. In the forenoon Dad, Mum and I went to Dinnet in the car. I walked down to Loch Kinord, and in the marsh at the west end sprang a fine roe with a large calf. On the loch swam nearly 100 wigeon and several hundred mallard, three goldeneyes and a great black-backed gull, and a heron fished at the edge. Red grouse were fairly plentiful on the moor, the cocks crowing loudly, nearly 20 in total as we drove along, mostly near the public road to the Burn o' Vat. I walked close to Loch Davan at its south-west end, where a pair of mute swans swam with a juvenile, and at the north-west corner I saw a flock of 11 drake

AW sen and AW at Allt Phouple, October 1946

AW in gale at Derry Cairngorm summit, 30 December 1946 (photo Adam Watson sen)

AW sen at Derry Cairngorm, 30 December 1946

AW at Little Cairngorm, 30 December 1946 (photo Adam Watson sen)

and two duck pochard, and packs of 400 wigeon and 200 mallard. Here there swam also a drake tufted duck, a few coots, and four singleton goldeneyes including two very fine adult drakes, an immature drake with a chocolate-coloured head, and an adult duck.

In the afternoon at Ballater, an adult pair of goosanders flew down Dee at the bridge, accompanied by a first-winter drake. I walked up Craigendarroch, seeing many capercaillie droppings in the upper half among the Scots firs. There was a fine wild view from the top, where I watched the sun go down behind Lochnagar and snow falling on the Glen Clova hills. Later we drove to Braemar in the evening, and below Creag Clunie saw a dozen red deer crossing the main road in our headlights, a fine sight. The Cairngorm Club had a meet at the Invercauld Arms in Braemar.

Chapter 5. 1947

1 January. Craig Coillich at Ballater

In the whins by the Ballater golf course I saw a few yellowhammers, and watched a goosander flying high as it followed the course of Dee upstream. In the afternoon I climbed Craig Coillich in a very strong wind, with stinging showers of sleet. Mist had come down on the hills.

2 January. Craig Coillich and Morrone

It was evidently pouring rain all last night till 7 this morning, but by 8.45 had turned clear and frosty. During the forenoon I again climbed Craig Coillich and saw three red grouse at the top. The snow had all melted up to 2000 feet, but the high hills had received a heavy plastering last night, with deep snow blown on to west-facing slopes. There was a very fine view, and at the foot of the hill I saw a big bird sailing over the trees on Craigendarroch. At first I thought it was a capercaillie, but it proved to be a common buzzard, and I got very good views of it as it sailed about.

In the early afternoon, Dad and I drove to Braemar in the car, seeing flocks of greenfinches and chaffinches in fields at Crathie, and then magnificent scenery with the snowy hills looking grand. After driving up Chapel Brae, we left the car at about 1300 feet, because beyond that the surface was solid ice. We began climbing at 1.40 and reached the summit cairn at 2.45. At first, solid ice covered the path, but soon changed to a heavy coating of hard snow above 2000 feet, whence very good going. At 2250 feet a large pack of nearly 60 red grouse flew past along the snowy slopes, and we flushed numerous other red grouse, some singing.

There was a magnificent view in all directions from the top, especially to Lochnagar and the Cairnwell hills. A bank of thick snow clouds was advancing on the west and central Cairngorms, which looked very wild and snowy indeed. The sun was glowing a warm pink on the snow slopes of Lochnagar, and Loch Callater was obviously under thick ice. Fine views also to Glas Maol, the Glen Ey hills, and others. At the summit of Morrone the cairn was thickly covered with frozen fog crystals and ice. After taking a few photographs we set off downhill.

I forgot to say that our Border terrier Duff climbed with us and seemed to enjoy himself immensely, running after grouse packs in flight, though shivering when we stopped at the cairn, for the air had become very frosty. We came down in 45 minutes, seeing several bullfinches in the trees at Tomintoul croft by the edge of the heather, and had tea at the Invercauld Arms. Parts of the river Dee were frozen below Braemar. At Coilacriech, a weasel ran across the road and a tawny owl sat on a telephone pole.

4 January. Morrone

I caught the 10 am bus from Ballater and walked up Chapel Brae to Morrone. The Dee in spate had burst its banks above and below Braemar, and a loch covered the marsh west of the village. Slight rain fell as I passed Tomintoul croft and at 2300 feet changed to snow, with an inch lying. I reached the top ¾ hour after leaving the bus, in dead silence except for continual ticking calls of red grouse in every direction. Cloud shrouded the Cairngorms, but I got magnificent views of Lochnagar and Glas Maol before mist closed in.

Along the ridge I walked south half a mile, saw many more grouse, and had fine glissading down a steep drift using my ice-axe. A hare ran out of a hole among rocks for a few feet and sat bolt upright, white save for blue-grey touches on its back. I approached and almost touched it before it ran ten yards to sit upright again. Snow fell heavily. In dense mist I descended, coming out of it at 1800 feet where 30 hinds and calves grazed the hillside. A blackcock stood in a treetop at Tomintoul, and many robins sang in Braemar, where I caught the 2 pm bus to Ballater.

24 March. News from Braemar

Today I got a letter from Eric Hosking, who plans to come with George Edwards for bird photography on Mar and asked me to help. I am looking forward to this greatly. George is due to come to Braemar by car on 27 March and I arranged for us to stay at Luibeg with James Beattie and Miss George, but Braemar Constable 'Smiler' Florence phoned to report "Arctic conditions and freezing almost every night. A snow plough battered from Braemar through to Linn of

Dee on 22nd, and Beattie hasn't been in Braemar for three weeks. The glen road is impassable, and Beattie goes by horse-drawn sledge to meet Morgan the post at the Black Brig. Even the road to the Linn is very bumpy and only a rapid thaw will allow George Edwards and you to get through". On the evening of the 25th, a warm day, I phoned Smiler, who said the road to the Linn was now bare of snow, though single lane still. On the 26th he said deep soft snow still filled the glens, snow was drifting on slopes from Braemar upwards, and Beattie's road had not been opened, so I wired George Edwards to cancel the trip meantime.

2 May. To Inverey

Dad and I left Turriff at 5 pm, and on the way to Braemar on a fine sunny evening had grand views of Lochnagar and the Cairngorms spotlessly white. In the evening we drove to Inverey and had a great crack till 10 o'clock with George Edwards and Eric Hosking who are staying at Concord. As we left, the sunset light struck the whole of snowy Ben Macdui with a ruddy glow. I have never seen the hills so beautiful.

3 May. In Glen Ey

A bitterly cold morning with a strong east wind blew as Dad drove his car up Glen Ey with George, Eric and me. Briefly the sun sparkled on the Ey Burn and on snowy hills shining silvery below black clouds. We had an exciting view of Beinn Iutharn Mhor spotless down to 2500 feet, its north ridge with a stupendous cornice hanging over and showing huge cracks, ready to avalanche. Climbing up screes, we saw a big fox walking along, yellowish in colour. I went to the top of a spur of An Socach and had some good glissades down snowy gullies. One steep face carried icicles up to five feet high in great masses, continually breaking off in the gale, and the Ey Burn was frozen over at a corner. Later we drove to Glen Lui, but by the time we reached the Black Brig a blizzard had begun. As we drank tea in the car, Beattie came past in his horse trap, and after a brief word with us he vanished into the storm towards Luibeg.

On 11 May 1947, AW sits with Border terrier Rex in Glen Ey (photo Adam Watson sen)

17 May. Loch Etchachan and Ben Macdui

A frost last night gave way to a hot day with a south-west breeze, cloudless except in the afternoon when a few clouds appeared. At the estate office Dad and I met Frank Scott. He said that the eagle parents at one eyrie last year fed nothing but rabbits to their young. We drove to Derry Lodge where we saw chaffinches, coal tits and a goldcrest. Crossbills called explosively in the spruces and we had close views of a fine cock and hen. One stag still had both old antlers, but most had lovely velvet, with the longest new furry antlers six inches long. A pair of oystercatchers called.

Up Glen Derry, coal tits are scarce this year. We heard five cuckoos calling and saw two others pursued by meadow and tree pipits. Several redstarts flitted in the wood. One wheatear did a song-flight, a lovely sight. About 180 deer grazed the flats of

Glen Derry and a hen merlin flew past. At Glas Allt Mor we had a grand view of an eagle over Coire an Lochain Uaine, beating up the screes. Snow filled all gullies where burns come down.

We came out at Loch Etchachan after seeing a total of 21 ptarmigan in pairs and single cocks. A deep continuous snow bridge covered the burn at its top, but occasionally a hole had appeared, with water frothing through the snow. Ice and snow completely hid Loch Etchachan, but had started to crack at the east end. From the loch to the summit we walked over snow for about half the way, very bright with the sun glaring. Big cornices lined the rim of Coire Sputan Dearg. A bitter wind blew on the summit, where we walked on hard snow. Views were magnificent, and we saw Lochnagar and Glas Maol, but haze obscured distant hills. Most of the Dee waterfall lay under snow, with immense drifts at the top and in the hole of the Garbh Choire Mor. We took four hours to go up, spending much time looking at birds and crossing burns, mostly over two feet above normal level because of melting snow.

After leaving at 2.15 we walked to the top above Coire Sputan Dearg. Here we met four walkers with shoes, sometimes up to their knees in soft snow. Then we descended beside enormous cornices ready to fall. One crevasse was ten feet deep, three feet wide and about 15 yards long. Ice and snowdrifts covered Lochan Uaine, but cracks had opened in the deep drift at one end. A very tame cock ptarmigan among boulders let us up to six feet and then flew off, snorting, and we saw a fine cock snow bunting. Awe-inspiring cornices ringed the cliff edges. We had tea at a rocky outcrop and then a good glissade down a long drift.

Below Sron Riach we crossed Luibeg Burn with difficulty, for the fast flood covered nearly all rocks. Occasional drifts lay at 1600 feet and enormous amounts on all high hills. Several ring ouzels and wheatears rose near the trees. A cuckoo called behind the now vacant Luibeg Cottage, where nobody was about, and a wheatear sang. We reached Derry Lodge at 5.25 on a lovely evening, but a bit spoilt by seeing one of our tyres flat.

A hen golden eagle flies off a nesting crag, 11 May 1947

30 June. Ben Macdui plateau

Warm and sunny. I cycled from Coylumbridge to Loch Morlich, where I met George Edwards and Eric Hosking. Leaving my bike at the saw-mill, I went in their car to Glenmore Lodge, picking up Dave Sergeant at his tent. George, Dave and I left at 10.30 and walked the path by Allt Mor, and then by a path to Allt Creag an Leth-choin. We climbed grassy slopes to the Miadan, with glorious views across to Coire an Lochain, which held enormous snow wreaths at the edge of the big granite slab. Big snow blocks had rolled in an avalanche off the slab to the foot of the corrie. A hind had a large calf on the Miadan.

Pleasant hours we spent on the plateau, looking for snow buntings and dotterel, and I ringed a brood of dotterel. We walked to the top of Ben Macdui and saw many craneflies on the gravel. At the top of the March Burn we came upon a snow tunnel eight feet high and 20 feet or more across, with the burn roaring down through it and melt-water dripping from the roof, which comprised a series of shallow hollows indented in the snow. The tunnel continued for 100 yards in a steep slope until the burn appeared at the foot. I had a fast standing glissade down the wreath.

Then we descended steep scree to the Lairig Ghru, and down the path. In the wood we took the track to Loch Morlich, arriving there tired at 8 pm after an 18-mile tramp, but one of the very best days I have ever spent in the Cairngorms.

2 July. My first crossing of the Lairig Ghru

A clear dry morning with a cool wind changed soon to wet misty weather. After breakfast at Mrs Garrow's, the house below the start of the Lairig path, I packed my rucksack and set off up at 8.35. In her Highland accent she said "You're very young for the Lairig". I had my first rest at the little tree on the last mound. Here a duck goosander flew up the burn, and I saw a few tree pipits, a tree creeper, spotted flycatchers and willow warblers in the last trees. Few old trees grow in these woods, which cannot compare with the woods of Mar for old firs, but have a healthy growth of young trees and juniper. I saw two roe deer down by Allt Druidh, but in the pass only wheatears and meadow pipits.

AW with Rex on Glas Maol, 19 May 1947 (photo Adam Watson sen)

After a last glance at Speyside still bright and clear, at 2500 feet I entered the mist and soon visibility dropped to 20 yards. At 11.35 I reached the summit where I saw a hen ptarmigan with five young as big as her, so they must have hatched early. Soon I came to the Pools of Dee. There I had lunch, fed the lean trout on a few crumbs, and left after noon. A thin drizzle began and at 2250 feet I came out of the mist. Above here a dead downy dotterel chick lay beside the path.

At Clach nan Taillear I met Dad who had walked to meet me. On the way to Luibeg we saw a greenshank, and in the firs a redstart and tree pipits. It became a foul day as we reached Luibeg at 3.30, I after 16 miles. Bob Scott is now at Luibeg, and we had a most welcome cup of tea from Mrs Scott before motoring down the glen.

20 July. Ben Macdui

Cloudless, south wind. At 3 pm I left Luibeg for Ben Macdui, carrying nothing but some food, map and compass, and flask of tea. Unburdened, I walked fast up the Sron Riach, stopping only for a cup of tea at the tor. Below the Sappers' Bothy, about 150 deer stood close to me in a thick mass, and later trooped in single file down Garbh Uisge Mor. I reached the top in two hours, including two short rests. From the summit I crossed the Snowy Corrie to Garbh Uisge Beag and beyond, looking for dotterel, snow buntings and ptarmigan, and returned north of the Coire Mor, seeing a flying young snow bunting. A hen ptarmigan with big young led them to a spring, where she took a long drink. I returned to the summit and had a cup of tea. The view was as good as I have ever seen it, with Ben Nevis and other hills sharp and clear. I sat in the sun, admiring the grand panorama until 6.30 and came to Luibeg at 8.30, after my first trip alone to Ben Macdui. It is the most interesting hill in the Cairngorms.

21 July. Leaving Luibeg

Rain poured most of the day. My Luibeg holiday ended today and it has been one of the best ever, with magnificent weather. In the forenoon I helped Bob Scott fit a new chimney to the bothy, which he has revolutionised since James Beattie's time. Some folk staying the weekend had a shooting brake and gave me a lift to Aberdeen, with a brief stop at Ballater where I sent my bike off by rail. They dropped me at Blackfriars Street, where a bus to Turriff came in a few minutes.

20 December. First long winter trip to Luibeg

For years I have wanted a long winter trip. Last week I asked schoolmate Stuart Conacher to come and he was keen, but his father forbade it because he thinks it's too risky. So I go on my own, which adds to the adventure. School holidays begin on the evening of the 23rd, but I'll not wait that time.

After a spot of breakfast I ran to catch the first train to Aberdeen. My class-mate Christine Imray was going to Glasgow on the first train and I accompanied her to Aberdeen. I had some time till the bus, so we had a cup of tea at the station, and then I walked up to Bon Accord Street to catch the 10 am bus to Braemar. I slept from Aberdeen to Banchory, and just at Banchory saw two magpies, one on a cow's back. I slept again from Banchory to Ballater, but woke up for a minute before Kincardine o' Neil, where I had a view of the east Cairngorms a very long way off, but clear, blue and splashed with snow. I slept again to Ballater. I enjoyed the bus journey from Ballater to Braemar thoroughly, for the colours were marvellous, though Lochnagar was nearly snow-free. Before Invercauld Bridge, Beinn a' Bhuird loomed through a gap in the trees, and it looked grand, with the Snowy Corrie and east corries full of snow, and the whole hill tinted beautifully.

It was turning out a superb day: quite cloudless. After hiring a bike in Braemar I cycled to Inverey, seeing 30 mallard in pairs on the river. In bracing cold air I reached Inverey in half an hour. There by the greatest stroke of luck I saw Bob Scott's pony and trap outside Mr Morgan's house, and Bob told me to shove in my ice-axe and rucksack. Eight ravens croaked loudly while flying over, their wings turned a golden sheen by the sun's rays, and a few crossbills called. Then I cycled to Luibeg, which I reached in good time. It was difficult to believe the date, for it seemed more like 20 May. The hills rose sharp and clear, and even Ben Macdui lacked unbroken snow. I had a stimulating view of Luibeg from the lodge, the smoke from the lum waving in the strong wind. Soon I stood at Luibeg, looking at the local group of 20 stags.

In the evening, two Glasgow mountaineers Tom Weir and Allan McNicol arrived to stay in the house for a few days. One, Tom Weir, a keen ornithologist and mountaineer, is a member of the Scottish Ornithologists' Club. Standing against the kitchen wall he held us all with his stimulating conversation.

21 December. With Tom Weir to Derry Cairngorm

A north-west gale blew with clouds and flying drizzle, which fell as sleet or snow high up. Tom, Allan and I left at 10 for Derry Cairngorm as a nice start to break us in, and saw a fine greyhen in the wood. Four ptarmigan flew off Carn Crom like bullets, and while having a rest at Little Cairngorm we heard a dull scream and saw the gale rip moss and earth to send them flying. Clouds skimmed Derry Cairngorm, but a hurricane blew at the summit, and we had to crawl on hands and knees for the last 20 yards to the cairn. Ice covered Lochan Uaine of Ben Macdui.

After crawling on hands and knees for the first 20 yards beyond the cairn, we walked to the next conical top and had to crawl there too. Then we walked to Loch Etchachan, frozen round the edges, where mist came close and snow flurries whirled past. After lunch and a drink from a burn we descended Coire Etchachan, seeing a raven. We reached Luibeg at 3 pm to find two more from Glasgow, pals of Allan's.

23 December. On Beinn a' Bhuird

At dawn, two stags stood at the rubbish tip, awaiting Bob's pail of food refuse. Five of us left at 9.40. We walked smartly through Clais Fhearnaig, where 40 stags grazed. Strangely, on seeing us they ran towards us, spreading in a fan, and stopped 100 feet off.

Descending to Glen Quoich, we saw about 70 hinds, red and in good condition. A snow bunting flew from a ditch, tame and with only a trace of white on its wings. Now blue sky appeared as we walked to An Diollaid. A deep drift lay beyond here, with 14 ptarmigan on it. They walked down the snow and flew, crossing the slope like whirling snowflakes. The snow had many roost hollows, filled to half an inch with droppings.

Next we climbed a broad grassy ridge beside a snowfield, and emerged at the Coire an Dubh-lochain cliffs. We crossed to the South Top for lunch and then returned north. Deep cornices hung on corries and ice floes floated on lochans. The sun felt quite warm. After reaching the North Top at 1 pm we traversed springs, frozen pools and hard snow to Cnap a' Chleirich, where we saw the sea. Poor weather prevailed west and south, with mist and rain. On the ridge to Stob an t-Sluichd we passed a deep hole of snow, found the remains of a crashed plane, and had good views of the Mitre Ridge.

With light failing, a strong wind faced us as we headed back. Snow clouds loomed to the west, so we hurried over the North Top and quickly descended to Moine Bhealaidh, seeing a few ptarmigan and snow buntings. On the moss we floundered in peat hags and coarse tussocks until 4.30. Cock grouse called in every direction at dusk.

Dusty Miller and I lost sight of the others, so we walked downhill. Two stags roared in Glen Derry. Beinn a' Chaorainn looked grand in the moonlight, a black cone with a crescent snowdrift. We met the others and came through the wood in moonlight, arriving tired but happy at 5.30 after 23 miles, one of my best hill days.

24 December. On Ben Macdui and Carn a' Mhaim

After 10 o'clock we set off for Ben Macdui. We had a nice view of it from the path, and quickly ascended the Sron Riach, seeing two snow buntings. After reaching the col and looking down to frozen Lochan Uaine where the ice had partly broken up, we climbed to the sharp peak above Coire Sputan Dearg beside a fine line of cornices. To the south and west, heavy clouds shrouded the hills. As we lunched on the cliff edge, 20 ptarmigan flew to alight near the loch.

Next we crossed to Ben Macdui past a large wreath in the Snowy Corrie, and saw more snow west and south-west of the top than anywhere else in the Cairngorms. We reached the top in time to look over shifting seas of grey-blue cloud stretching from Lochnagar to Ben Rinnes. Big walls of cloud kept drifting over Braeriach and Cairn Toul, down into the Lairig Ghru and then up fast in strong air currents, leaving Ben Macdui clear. We had fine views to Speyside, Aberdeenshire and the North Sea. Then we descended to the Carn a' Mhaim col as the clouds cleared.

Quickly we walked along the ridge, and on the way saw a big flock of ptarmigan fly across to Coire Clach nan Taillear, followed by scores more, at least 250 altogether. On the ridge, a ptarmigan let me approach to ten feet, still not in winter plumage, with a wholly grey back and grey patches on either side, and a little grey on the head. Ptarmigan rose in little flocks on the ridge, looking like white doves, especially in flight against the dark slopes.

Then a pair of golden eagles flew within a minute to Sron na Lairige and into the clouds. They flew into the strong wind, yet did not move their wings. Next a second pair appeared from Glen Luibeg and vanished into Glen Geusachan,

Luibeg in moonlight, 26 December 1947

raising 50 ptarmigan, which shot off in alarm. On the shoulder of Carn a' Mhaim we had a short glissade down a snow slope and arrived at Luibeg before dark.

25 December. Glen Derry

We awoke to find an inch of snow. After breakfast, Bob and I walked up the Derry. It snowed most of the time, but melted in the glen. Over the east trees we saw a raven and a fine eagle. We did a round of the fox traps and at one trap flushed a nice bright little common snipe, which Bob says has been at this pool for a few weeks. It was sitting on a bone of a deer carcase when we saw it. Bob and I walked up to the Derry Dam and back along the east side, with lovely views of the Cairngorms between showers, and Beinn Bhrotain gleaming with a bright rosy colour in the sun. We saw parties of stags moving down to the woods and flushed a hen capercaillie.

In the plantation the eagle appeared again, we saw two roe deer and Bob shot one roe after a short stalk. Both of them ran like the wind. We thought he had missed, but found the roe dying 200 yards down the wood, a lovely beast. Shot in a lung, it had run fast at first. We carried it to the lodge. I got a surprise to see Dad's car at the lodge and found him at Luibeg. Two chaps came to the bothy from the Shelter Stone today, quite exhausted after struggling in the snow. At 9 pm, Tom, Allan, Dad and I went out to photograph the snowy glen in moonlight.

27 December. First day on skis

It snowed heavily when we rose and six inches lay. Dad feared the gale would return and blow snow to block the road, so after breakfast he drove to Braemar. Ice had formed on the Luibeg Burn and many stags grazed in the wood or rested in the snow.

Allan and Tom went out skiing on seven inches of snow and I accompanied them on Allan's spare pair, my first time on skis. I found walking easy, but uphill and downhill difficult. Often I fell. Then we crossed to the hillocks, where I went further on the slope each time without falling, guided by Tom's jovial shouts "Bend your knees" and other instructions, his face in a wide grin.

When Tom and I went out at 3, the surface had turned sticky and heavy going. On the way to the lodge we had a fine view of four golden eagles. They raised a cock capercaillie which flew over fast, and then one eagle - a big hen - flew close to us at treetop height, while the others soared up the glen. On wet snow we skied up the Derry, round the wood to the Lairig Ghru path, next my first run from the top of the hillock without falling, and then through wet snow to Luibeg. Frost set in after sleet, and the clouds cleared to show perfect moonlight on nine inches of snow.

28 December. First ski-tour

The snow had a hard crust this morning, though not enough to bear one's weight. On skis we left early for the shoulder of Carn a' Mhaim. By now, the black clouds had vanished to leave mere puffs of creamy cloud on the highest tops. A bitter wind blew but skiing is no cold sport. We found a lovely slope of velvety drifted snow, ran on it for a while, and lunched.

Above 2750 feet the snow had drifted yesterday, leaving exposed tops looking grey because of their boulders, though deep snow filled lee slopes. Soon we came down to the wooden bridge and I had some lovely long runs without falling. On foot, we sank to the knees at every step. Allan and Tom went up Carn Crom on skis and down to the lodge, which I thought too steep for a novice, so I skied downhill most of the way to Luibeg. I enjoyed this run best of all so far, and at the Sands o Lui the sun came out brilliantly for a few minutes on sparkling snow.

From Luibeg I skied to the lodge, where 100 stags stood at the burn. Up the glen I met Allan and Tom, and we returned to the hillocks for a few runs. A frost set in, with stags right down to the house. A pink halo circled the moon, and further out was a white halo with a radius 25 times the moon's diameter, a sign of bad weather.

29 December. Skiing on Sgor Dubh

It dawned clear with some clouds. We set off up Sgor Dubh, carrying skis to the skyline ridge, and then skied to the summit. For a mile to the south we had fast skiing on perfect powder snow. We returned to the cairn five times and ran down again each time. While we had lunch, a raven barked as it flew over. The sky became stormier as black clouds piled over Beinn a' Ghlo, whose slopes had turned inky blue. Tom said the run was the best he had ever had, better even than in Norway. I did it most times without falling, and thought it wonderful to move so easily on snow.

Tom and Allan skied towards Sgor Mor, while I decided to ski a shorter distance towards Glen Lui. I had some lovely running, and once saw the sun sparkling on snow at Bynack Lodge. On gradual slopes I skied on some hard parts where skis left no marks, followed by velvety-soft drifts. At one burn I fell through a cornice and head-first into a soft drift. I took several minutes to extricate myself, for I could barely reach my bindings to loosen them. Then I skied to Glen Lui, fast over hillocks, slopes and tall heather covered with snow. I fell a few times due to rough going.

As I skied quickly towards stags grazing on the old army football pitch they paid little or no attention, and I was right among them before they ran. Fox tracks marked the snow at one point on Feith nan Sgor, and on this side of Glen Lui two fox tracks in parallel continued to a hillock opposite the lodge. There I saw a stag with curious antlers, one normal and the other sticking down. He rubbed the odd one on a boulder as I approached, and then trotted off, shaking his head. Now to the south-east the sky turned yellow and black, but cleared up the Lairig. I came to Luibeg from the south-east after a fine long day on ski, the most enjoyable day I have ever had.

Allan and Tom arrived later. While changing a ski binding, Allan's skis pointed downhill. One hurtled off to crack on a boulder, an expensive ski which Allan had bought in Norway. Disappointed when he came in, he sat gloomily, and said "I wish it had been my leg. You can at least mend a leg but you can't mend a ski." A light snow dusting fell and the moon had a white halo. From outside, the bothy fire and light sparkled through a row of icicles outside the window.

30 December. Views from Sgor Dubh

Next morning we awoke to a severe frost. The Luibeg Burn had frozen over in large stretches and a heavy deposit of frost coated the long blades of grass and the old firs. A wee wren fluttered round the hen-house and I saw the dunnock again and photographed Beattie the tame old stag, standing in the snow. After breakfast, the sun rose and we went out to the bridge. Carn a' Mhaim and Carn Crom glowed a soft rosy colour in the first sun-rays, with Beinn Bhreac tinted dull rose and bright blue alternately. Gaining power, the sun flooded the Carn Crom firs and frost glittered like diamonds on grass blades. As the blades moved softly in the light breeze, the shifting diamonds produced a scene of sparkling splendour. At the bridge, thick ice hid the burn and a little trout moved under a thin sheet of ice.

We set off to climb Sgor Dubh, I carrying an ice-axe, and Allan and Tom skis. Now that Allan had broken a ski, he took his spare pair that I had used. Snow buntings twittered on the north-facing slope where the midwinter sun never shines. After reaching the top ridge I sank to the ankles at every step and sometimes to the knees, but eventually reached the cairn, and Tom and Allan came up on skis, on snow even better than yesterday. A weak sun topped Beinn Iutharn Mhor and turned the ridges between it and Sgor Dubh to rippling silver. The foreground snow sparkled softly, and miles of sparkling snow stretched to the upper Feshie. I have never seen hills look so cold and yet so beautiful, as An Sgarsoch and Carn an Fhidhleir under heavy snow.

Skiing towards Linn of Dee, Allan and Tom had soon gone a mile, out of sight. I sat half an hour at the cairn to admire the view. Snow clouds wreathed Cairn Toul, with its two aretes of Coire an t-Sabhail leading to a cone rising out of clouds. Big cornices hung above Coire an Lochain Uaine of Derry Cairngorm. Bright buff-coloured snow covered the slopes of Beinn a' Chaorainn and Beinn Mheadhoin, quite extraordinary.

A barking raven flew over and 30 red grouse alighted near the cairn, clucking excitedly. Scanned with binoculars, I saw at Geldie 100 deer, at Bynack 150, and on Creag an Lochain in Glen Ey at least 200. Other herds moved uphill to high ridges, a sign of temperature inversion.

After a last glance over the long sparkling slopes and ski tracks to the cairn and fast-sinking sun, I walked to the top of the steep slope and slid in a sitting glissade. I had a spot of lunch at Luibeg, which I left at 3 o'clock just as a snowstorm began. Bob had taken our packs by horse and cart to Mar Lodge and I met him at Derry Lodge on his return. He said a tractor and trailer had just been at the lodge with hay, so I cycled at top speed on the rough icy tracks, caught up with the tractor, and the driver stopped a moment to let me mount the trailer. Heavy snow now fell. Stags grazed Glen Lui, with lines of them on hillsides and black like ants on the glen floor, and some hinds and calves. The total including a small herd at the Black Brig and some at the lodge numbered over 500. A rough journey followed to Mar Lodge.

There I took my pack, bicycle and the broken pair of skis, and cycled parts and slipped other parts on icy roads to Braemar at 4.30. There I met Tom and Allan, and caught the 5 pm bus to Ballater, the end of the best holiday I have ever had in my life.

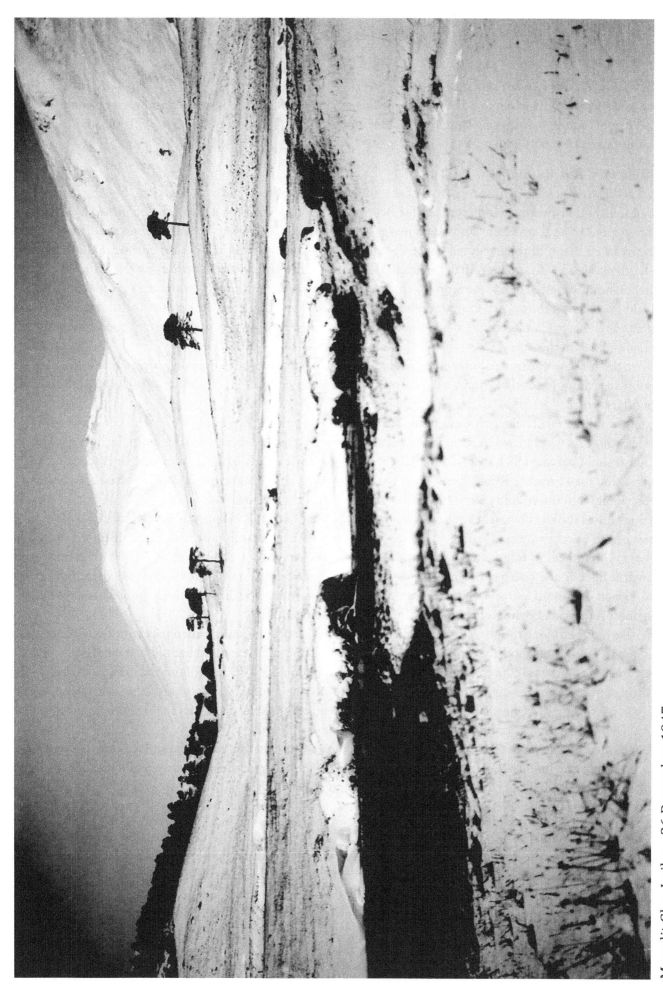

Moonlit Glen Luibeg, 26 December 1947

Chapter 6. 1948

7 February. Buying our first skis

Dad and I went to Aberdeen to buy two pairs of skis, sticks and skins. Skis have been unprocurable until the army released surplus equipment after pressure by ski clubs, and Campbell's Rubber Shop now has 160 pairs. They cost £9 per pair of skis, sticks and skins.

13 February. Ben Macdui

Dad and I woke at Luibeg to see an overcast sky, snow above 2200 feet, and a crossbill in a fir. After breakfast the sun appeared, and in clearing weather we left for Ben Macdui at 10.15. A cock eagle with a light patch on each wing raised two grouse over Carn Crom, and a dark hen eagle flew low at Sands o Lui. By now the sun shone brightly, silver clouds wreathed Beinn Bhrotain, and in Coire Creagach an immense drift lay below a big cornice. Soon Ben Macdui rose ahead, plastered with snow. From the Sands to the Sron Riach a fox had left footprints on the path.

After an hour we rested below the Sron Riach. The sun's heat was astonishing, we wore dark goggles because of the glare, and I had only a thin jacket above my jersey. On hard snow and soft drifts we reached the tor, where we looked west to an impressive Cairn Toul, its ridges lined by shadows. Here we saw 50 snow buntings, two ptarmigan and a third eagle golden in the sun.

Above the tor rose a furrowed snow slope, and above Lochan Uaine a cliff draped greyish-white in ice and snow, with snow sparkling gloriously. Beyond, a diffuse mist spread over Ben Macdui. Enormous cornices lined the cliff edge, almost 50 feet thick.

So far the weather had held with a warm sun, but clouds now engulfed Braeriach. We lunched on the corrie edge at 3750 feet, where no wind stirred. A cornice hung in a long tongue ten feet long, and to the south the hills sparkled with silver in the sun. Carrying much spare clothing because we had expected a blizzard, by the time we reached the plateau we had to stop for a breather. Rime draped every rock at the peaky top. It was eerie to stand on the big flat rock at the topmost point, with the visibility ten feet, aware of the 1000-feet drop below.

In thick mist I took a compass bearing for the summit. We seemed to walk a long way over the plateau, with only the slightest breath of cool wind and visibility three to five yards. I have never seen mist so dense. It distorted every object in sight, so I used Dad in front as a mark. With relief I saw the ruin of the Sappers' Bothy, 100% direction finding. A snowdrift filled it and two feet of rime covered the sides. Beyond, rime up to three feet thick covered the cairn. It looked like an enormous snowman, the indicator being like a mushroom with rime projecting all round. I scraped through soft rime crystals with a glove and saw hill names underneath.

Then we returned along the plateau, still in thick mist as I took a bearing and counted paces until near the top above Coire Sputan Dearg, and another bearing to Loch Etchachan. We heard not a sound but the crunch of boots on frozen snow or their rasping squeaks in fresh drifts. Rime covered every boulder. We came out of the mist at 3800 feet. Then, each sitting on an oilskin gas-cape and wielding an ice-axe to steer and brake, we glissaded to the loch, frozen and deep under snow. Crossing it, we hurried on, as the sun had gone and snow clouds darkened the sky. Where the burn leaves the loch, Dad fell through a continuous snow bridge into the burn.

We glissaded on gas-capes down Coire Etchachan, seeing a few ptarmigan, and then walked down Glen Derry in snow softened by the sun. It was dark when we reached Luibeg at 6.30, after four hours up and four hours back. Mist must have added over an hour to our time. It had been a grand day on the hill, and if the sun had kept shining would have been easily my best day ever.

14 February. First day on our own skis

A morning with mist to 1800 feet and pelting rain. As I woke, I saw through the window a raven fly over. It rained hard all forenoon, but after 1 in moderate rain we walked up Sgor Dubh, carrying ex-army skis bought last week in Aberdeen. At the skyline we entered the mist, but came upon continuous snow and put on our skis. The old snow had turned almost into ice, but the skins held and soon we reached the top. On the east side stretched a slope where hard

Moonlit Bad an t-Seabhaig, 26 December 1947 (photo Adam Watson sen)

icy snow alternated with soft slushy-like snow. We had to shove the skis forward on the slushy snow and then suddenly they shot off on the ice. Braking was almost impossible on the icy snow because the ski edges would not bite. We practised here for a while, until visibility fell to 20 yards. Some good ski runs led to the edge above Luibeg, one of 300 yards fast on icy snow. Dad enjoyed his first day on ski. For a few minutes blue sky appeared above, but mist soon closed in again. When we came out of it, the light was gloomy. A few snow buntings rose at the wood edge.

15 February. Skiing in a circle on Creagan nan Gabhar

Dull again this morning. Carrying Bob's potato peelings, I photographed Beattie the tame stag. As I approached, he barked and ran off, but when I tipped out the peelings he came close to eat. Then I heard a metallic noise and turned to see two stags fighting. Rushing at one another, they clashed antlers. Then one got his antlers on to the other's side and chased it for 100 yards.

At 10 we left for Glen Luibeg carrying skis. Mist draped the Glen Geusachan cliffs, making them look higher than usual. As we reached Lochan Feith nan Sgor we sweated in mild humid air, and shortly the mist fell to 1750 feet and drizzle started. We planned to ski from Creagan nan Gabhar to Sgor Mor and Sgor Dubh, and thought we would not need a compass on such a low ridge. At 2000 feet we strapped on skis and ascended to Creagan nan Gabhar. Here a great drift at 45° angle lay over the rocks, with soft snow above a frozen layer, so I kicked steps to the top, where we had a fine drink of cold water from a pot hole in a tor.

By now the mist had cut visibility to 15 yards. We skied down in zigzags and then uphill for nearly a mile to a rocky outcrop. Beyond rose a snow slope, obviously the last slope to Sgor Mor I thought. Now at 1 o'clock, we decided to save time by skipping the top of Sgor Mor and skiing below it to Sgor Dubh. We skied for a mile over long rolling slopes, and in front rose a snowy slope with rocks at the top. Ah! I thought, the outcrop between Sgor Mor and Sgor Dubh. But, as we skied up, suddenly I noticed ski tracks in front. For a second I stood staring blankly, wondering who would ski here on such a bad day, and then in a flash realised they were my tracks. What an ass I felt! We had gone in an anti-clockwise circle for over two miles. Had we walked, this would not have happened. We had learned how hard it is to navigate in a straight line when skiing in zigzags downhill in mist, and how vigilant one must be when doing so.

Tired and covered in mist droplets, we sat at the top of Creagan nan Gabhar. Time had flown. We put on skis, and I brought my rather shaken sense of direction into action, now concentrating on it totally. I led on ski for half a mile down to some springs, obviously leading to a burn running out of the Black Corries into the Luibeg Burn. We followed the snow-covered burn for half a mile and had some fine ski running, but my ski-stick stuck in heather while I skied downhill, I could not release my hand in time, and the wooden stick snapped at the foot. After coming out of the mist, we carried skis in pouring rain down to the Luibeg Burn, waded across, and then walked down the path to Luibeg, which we reached at 3, hungry and soaked. Then we packed up and drove to Turriff. A grand weekend, and I thoroughly enjoyed it despite the bad weather.

8 March. At school at Turriff
Today was the warmest this year, up to 60 F, so I hope it doesn't melt all the snow.

9 March. Ready for going to Luibeg
Temperature well over 60 F. I am apprehensive about the snow. Tonight I packed my rucksack for Luibeg, and look forward to going on the hill again with Tom Weir.

10 March. To Luibeg
Woke at 6.30 this morning, clear sky, and caught the first train for Aberdeen. On Don at Kintore I saw nine whooper swans including a cygnet. Then I took a bus up Deeside, and was relieved to see some snow on the high hills. I arrived at Braemar at 12.45 and walked with a heavy pack to the Linn of Dee. It was cloudless until 1 pm, with the sun shining nicely on Lochnagar, but later cloudy with a strong north-west wind. Beinn a' Bhuird looked particularly fine through the trees at Corriemulzie, with snow bulging out in the Snowy Corrie. I arrived at the Linn in 1¾ hours and met stalker Jock Stewart. In his shed I got Bob Scott's bicycle and cycled up the glen.

A mile up, a bicycle lay at the side of the road and as I cycled past I heard a shrill whistle. I stopped, thinking it would be Tom Weir, and, sure enough, his red and white woollen cap appeared out of the heather in a second or two! He has been in the Cairngorms for a week, skiing back and fore from Coylum to Luibeg, and one day skied over Braeriach and Cairn Toul to Glen Geusachan, where he left his skis. The snow has taken a big shake with the heat of the last two days, but today up Glen Derry he saw fresh snow dusting the tops. We cycled to Luibeg and then walked up Sgor Dubh. At the top a tearing west gale blew and mist enshrouded the high hills.

Tom and I had a great crack in the evening. On Sunday he heard a snow bunting singing in the flock, and has seen two golden plovers high up. A pair of oystercatchers has arrived at Luibeg. On Sunday he tried to go to Speyside, but had to turn when falling snow and mist cut visibility to his ski tips. He saw several slopes of ice in the Garbh Choire and has had a grand time. He suggested we go up Geusachan tomorrow, ski on the top, and he would go to Spey while I returned to Luibeg. The prospect really excites me. A fine starry night bodes well for tomorrow.

11 March. On Braeriach and Cairn Toul
We woke at 6.30 at Luibeg, to find blue sky, chaffinches singing, crossbills feeding, and an eagle flying past. Three yellowhammers, two cocks and a hen, sat on the fence outside the window. None of us had seen them here before, so probably they are migrating.

After breakfast we left at 7.45, each carrying one of my skis, for Tom had dumped his in Glen Geusachan on Sunday. The sky had become overcast and cloud hid Monadh Mor, but we hoped the strong wind would keep the cloud high. I found a half-crown coin on the side of Carn a' Mhaim and we thought this a token of luck.

We crossed Dee at the only feasible spot, an island below Devil's Point, and even here had to take time and make long jumps. Then we walked up Glen Geusachan, below slopes scarred by past watercourses. After picking up Tom's skis we walked up rough ground, snow bridges, and bogs. I spotted a robin at 2750 feet, chirping as it flitted in snow-filled peat hags, an amazing sight. Like the yellowhammers, probably it was migrating. Soon we saw a few snow buntings and ptarmigan in twos and threes, the cock ptarmigan showing dark speckling. They fluttered up to one another, clucking like corks coming out of bottles, and strutted with fanned tails.

On snow we walked where Allt Clais an t-Sabhail roared down over rocks, and climbed unbroken snow to Sgor an Lochain Uaine. Westwards a narrow line of blue broke the clouds, and by the time we reached Garbh Choire Mor at noon it had spread. The change came rapidly and ¼ hour later the sun shone from a cloudless sky. Cloud hid the lower slopes of hills to the west, and Tom identified them for me. It was the best view we have ever had in the Cairngorms.

From Sgor an Lochain Uaine past Monadh Mor to Ben Lawers, 18 March 1948

We parted, Tom to ski to Coire Dhondail and walk down Gleann Einich to Coylumbridge. After a snack I left my pack and skis, and walked on screes to Cairn Toul, wearing only a jersey above my shirt. The view from Cairn Toul surpassed that from Sgor an Lochain Uaine, and I sat in warm sunshine for ¾ hour enjoying it. Scotland seemed at my feet. Muirburn smoke rose from Deeside to the Monadh Liath. Clouds fell on a sharply clear Ben Nevis and the Glencoe hills peeped out of mist. Over the Cairngorms the sky was cloudless save for a few spear-shaped clouds shot with silver. Almost unbroken glistening snow covered Monadh Mor and Moine Mhor, and avalanche debris stained the snow of Coire Creagach. Beside me hung a cornice above Coire an t-Sabhail. On Garbh Choire Mor a cornice crashed down the cliff with a roar, sending blocks of snow up to 25 feet long racing down steep snow to pile up at the bottom. Returning to Sgor an Lochain Uaine, I marvelled at the enormous snow bulge at the col above the loch. I thought of Class V at their history examination at the school in Turriff, and was glad I had decided not to take the history course.

At Sgor an Lochain Uaine I slipped on my skis. Below me stretched an unbroken snow slope of two miles, half a mile wide. I seemed to float through the air with a thousand silvery peaks for company. The skis moved fast enough for me to see the hills changing position as I descended, something I always find fascinating on a ski-tour. The only sound was the crackle of the skis. In ten minutes I came to Loch nan Stuirteag in a wonderful run. After a snack, I skied over the east end of the Moine Mhor, up to the north top of Monadh Mor and down to the loch. The loch lay in the centre of a basin of unbroken snow. Here I practised some time and then at 4 o'clock decided to go. I climbed to the col for a last view. Light was fading over the Moine Mhor and the snowfields flushed warmly in the sun. The wind had long dropped, and intense silence and calm pervaded the rolling tablelands and snow slopes. I skied down to Lochan nan Stuirteag, frozen and covered in deep snow, and left my skis at the edge.

Then I walked down Glen Geusachan. At the grassy flats I sat for ¼ hour. The glen lay in shadow but the cliffs of the Devil's Point shone warmly in the sun. The snowy ridge of Monadh Mor gleamed bright gold. The burn hurried over shingle beds, and I could have stayed long enough listening to it and watching the varying spears of silver light on the cornices of Monadh Mor. I rose and walked down, seeing a twite and a pair of golden plover. I crossed Dee with no small difficulty, for it had risen since morning and each long jump from boulder to boulder had to cross a roaring flood. The climb to Carn a' Mhaim shoulder seemed interminable, and already I had covered 20 miles with some tough going. By now, the last sun-rays struck only the highest tops, turning the ridge of Cairn Toul golden and the screes of Ben Macdui warm red.

When I reached Luibeg Burn the snow on Ben Macdui was still glowing warm pink in the afterglow, although dusk had come to the glen. How fine to come through the old firs again. I reached Luibeg in the dark at 7.15 after almost 12 hours and 23 miles on the hill, and the very best day I have ever had.

9 April. Cairn Toul

Last night heavy snow fell on the hills. After Dad and I left Luibeg for Cairn Toul, hail fell but the sun came out. In Coire Odhar about nine inches of fresh snow had fallen above 2200 feet, and diamond sparkles on snow crystals caught the sun. At the top of the corrie we sank to the knee at each step and the sun beat strongly, but at the Buidheanach a bitter wind met us, sending hail showers into the Lairig. We kept to the exposed ridge to avoid heavy wading, and at the Slichit had a grand view of Cairn Toul shining in the sun and plastered by last night's blizzard. Here I stood on frozen old grey snow with a soft drifted cornice edge 15 feet away. Noticing a crack in the soft snow a yard away, I gently touched it with my axe spike while standing on the secure hard snow. Within a second came a dull loud 'plump' and the cornice of fresh snow for a length of 15 yards toppled into Coire an t-Saighdeir. Smartly I moved back, but I knew that the old grey snow was firm and reliable.

We climbed to the summit as the sun burst out from clouds and flooded all the Cairngorms. Frozen fog crystals plastered the cairn and to the west we could see all the hills clear, especially Clach Leathad and Ben Nevis, the last looking splendid. Showers of hail shrouded some hills from time to time, but the view was excellent. Far to the north, great ranges of snow-clad peaks at the top of Glen Affric rose into the sky. We walked to Sgor an Lochain Uaine, seeing stupendous cornices, especially at the col above frozen Lochan Uaine. On return we stopped at the Slichit for a last look at one of our best Cairngorms views, and then descended velvety snow to the lip above Coire Odhar. Here a

Braeriach from the col west of Cairn Toul, 18 March 1948

ptarmigan pair fed on plants, the hen quite yellow already. Trying to glissade proved useless because of soft snow, so we ran down in big strides.

For a while we sat in the sun outside Corrour Bothy, where meadow pipits filled the air with song and I spotted my first ring ouzel this year. Then we crossed Dee and rounded Carn a' Mhaim. From there I climbed into the east-facing cliffs and had an exhilarating standing glissade down a long snow-filled gully. As I left the cliff foot, a falling boulder crashed into the cliff with a loud shot, and, splitting into fragments, whistled right above me, with two big lumps passing only a few yards away. Soon I met Dad having a rest in Glen Luibeg, where we had grand views looking back to the hills. We arrived at Luibeg at 6 after my second best Cairngorms day so far. Tonight the oystercatchers called loudly and a tawny owl hooted in the wood.

14 May. Skiing in the Snowy Corrie

In the morning, mist lay to 2500 feet and I helped Bob saw logs. Towards 10.30 a touch of blue appeared to the west and at once I left for Ben Macdui carrying skis. A cuckoo sang in the Luibeg wood, once giving 15 calls in succession, and another at Preas nam Meirleach, where tree pipits sang and a pair of grey wagtails flitted at the burn. Now the sun broke through and the first view of Ben Macdui from the path sent a thrill through me, the granite boulders glowing warm red in the sun, contrasting with snowy cliffs. Here an eagle flew high and soon another soared from Coire Sputan Dearg to perform a spectacular diving display. With a strong wind behind it, in a series of climbs and dives it shot very fast round Carn Crom. Some dives with closed wings were breathtaking and the speed on most dives must have been over 100 mph.

Lochan Uaine had some ice floes and looked cool with the sun catching little waves. After walking to the cairn of Ben Macdui, I had two fine runs from the Sappers' Bothy down the Snowy Corrie to a spring, and then a swift rush down to the lochans. Although the sun vanished after noon, I spent a grand three hours skiing, and a snow bunting sang continually. I saw a hen with another singer, and four ptarmigan pairs.

Eventually I left, seeing big cornice remains at Sputan Dearg. I whooped with joy when I saw a beautiful ski-run from the edge of the crags down to a lochan, ending with a curve round the water's edge. As the sun appeared again, the lochan sparkled with silver. After a dozen runs, I left the skis and walked down by Derry Cairngorm.

There I found eight ptarmigan pairs. Always I saw the cock first, who snorted, fanned his tail and shuffled his wings. Then I saw the hen, who flew as I came near, with the cock following her. He was obviously drawing my attention. One hen had made a rough scrape and sat in it. The sun kept shining and an eagle caught the light as it circled the Sputan Dearg crags. I arrived at Luibeg at 7 after a fast descent. A glorious sunset behind Monadh Mor promised a good day tomorrow.

16 May. Cairn Toul and Braeriach

A marvellous day again. Leaving for Cairn Toul and Braeriach at 9.45, I walked quickly to Corrour, by which time a hot day had set in. At the Buidheanach a lovely dotterel fed at a pool. I reached Cairn Toul at 12.45 and sat for ¼ hour eating sandwiches. At Sgor an Lochain Uaine, four Aberdeen walkers with big packs said "Beer, lad, where is it?" so I pointed to a spring nearby. Many deer lay on the Monadh Mor snows, and I watched a snow bunting in song flight. I have never felt so fit and soon stood at the top of the Garbh Choire cliffs, here showing fantastic shattered patterns, with grottoes in the big gully cornices. A cold gale rushed up here, blowing from the snowfield below. The snow had moved away from the cliff edge, and cracks ribbed and edged the snowfield's centre like a miniature glacier. At Einich Cairn I sat for ¼ hour enjoying a beautiful view, with Speyside and Aviemore shimmering in the heat, the Culbin Sands, the Caithness hills rising from fog over the Moray Firth, and the Affric and Glen Shiel peaks splashed heavily with snow. Ben Nevis flaunted high above a score of intervening ridges.

As I strode to the Wells of Dee the heat became intense, and for half an hour I sat at the spring bubbling out of a snowdrift. It was hard to realise this was Scotland, so much did the snow-splashed plateau resemble Arctic tundra. I reached Braeriach top at 4, and later had a marvellous standing glissade at about 10 mph for 300 feet down Coire Ruadh on lovely snow.

For a time now I thought of returning over Ben Macdui. I felt so fit today that if I had left earlier , which I cursed myself for not doing, I could have climbed the four big tops taking plenty of time.

South-west from Cairn Toul, 18 March 1948

A rapid walk followed down the path, with grand views of Cairn Toul and Garbh Choire in lovely blue shadow and the sun really burning strongly in the Lairig pass. I wore shorts today, and my sunburned legs felt sore as heather brushed them, so I vowed to wear long trousers on sunny summer days, especially over snow. As I reached Luibeg after 7, sandpipers called at the burn and crossbills in the firs, at the end of as good a day as I have ever had.

5 June. Camp in a snowstorm on Ben Macdui

Dad and I arranged to meet Prof Wynne-Edwards at Luibeg, to camp on Ben Macdui. We reached Luibeg at 6 pm, followed by Wynne, his daughter Janet and son Hugh, and Mrs Scott gave us tea. Bob said it snowed on the hill every day last week. The weather looked poor, but we left at 6.40 with heavy loads. I walked ahead fast, unwilling to slacken to the others' slow speed, and had grand views of Cairn Toul where a sunbeam lit a white cloud.

Soon I entered mist. Above Lochan Uaine, huge wet snowflakes fell, none less than half-crown size, and shortly changed to stinging hail. I had no compass but easily reached the plateau at 8.50 in thick mist and a snowstorm. A bitterly cold wind blew, and by the time I erected the tent for a bivouac my fingers were numb, so I fixed the last buttons with my teeth. Inside, I soon warmed up and lit the stove. After half an hour I wondered if the rest had gone down, so I walked to the Sappers' Bothy and the summit, and then back to the top above Coire an Lochain Uaine. I met them coming up 300 feet below, and then we went to my bivouac. Just then the mist cleared and the sun shone with sudden intense brilliance through a hole in the mist. Hills beyond the Moray Firth rose sharp and clear, while the Snowy Corrie held a great amount of snow.

We moved to less exposed grass at the foot of the Snowy Corrie. Between here and the Sron Riach we had seen ten cock ptarmigan and Wynne found a sitting hen. After erecting the tents we drummed up hot OXO and soon became warm in our sleeping bags.

6 June. Summer snowstorm on Ben Macdui

What a night. The tent groaned, banged and shuddered though weighed down with boulders. I slept fitfully till 3 am, when I looked out to find a blizzard blowing, three inches of snow lying, a gale, and mist cutting visibility to ten yards. Crawling into my sleeping bag, I fell into a deep sleep lasting till 8.30, when I peeped out to see wet snow falling heavily. The snow falling on the tent melted, but although we touched the roof dozens of times, not a drop came in. However, Wynne's expensive Arctic tent leaked freely and water soaked everything inside.

After a quick breakfast we packed up. Dad and I left for the Sron Riach, while Wynne took an easier but longer route downhill by Loch Etchachan. As we climbed to the plateau, the snow became dry and stinging, and the mist thick. I had no map or compass, but found navigation easy. Two ptarmigan croaked and a snow bunting sang. A strong gale blew on the plateau, where four inches of snow lay. We descended the Sron Riach quickly, and reached Luibeg in heavy rain at noon, two and a half hours from camp. Mrs Scott gave us a fine meal, and her hospitality is unbounded. The Wynne-Edwards trio arrived very wet at 2, and Wynne said he saw a black throated diver on Loch Etchachan. We all left Luibeg at 4 and came home in bucketing rain. My ex-American army tent performed well and I would safely put it anywhere now.

11–12 June. The four highest Cairngorms

At 10 o'clock we reached Luibeg on a magnificent still night, cloudless and with a touch of frost, and over cups of tea Dad and I decided to walk all night over Braeriach and Cairn Toul. We left at 11.45, lightly burdened. Under a small yellow moon we soon reached the Carn a' Mhaim shoulder. It began to be darker as we descended to Corrour, and we noticed white fog in Glen Tilt. Crossing Dee proved tricky, because for quarter of an hour after 1 o'clock we could not see well. We made good progress up to the Slichit. Not the faintest breath of wind stirred in quite warm air. We heard not a sound save the continuous rushing of burns in the Lairig, a ptarmigan croaking in Coire an t-Saighdeir and a ring ouzel's fluty notes from velvety shade.

Cairn Toul we reached at 3.15, and here the silence and sense of solitude deepened. In the north-north-east the sky flushed red with the glow of the sun below the horizon and in Deeside dense cloud carpeted the strath and low hills, broadening eastwards like a river entering the sea. After walking to the Garbh Choire, we had a wonderful sensation as if walking on air as we strode over the high plateau to the Wells of Dee. Just beyond, I almost stood on a richly coloured ptarmigan with golden and black plumage, which allowed me to stroke her, and then suddenly flew 25 yards and ran out of sight behind a mound. She almost knocked one of her four eggs out of the nest. Very pale, they were almost pure white with a ring of brown spots round the big end. As we left the nest we heard loud fluting and a pair of dotterel flew fast high up, corkscrewing.

I raced to Braeriach top, as the sun would rise at any moment. Breathless, I had just reached the cairn when a ray of gold appeared above the cloud sea to the north-east and touched the summit cairn and Cairn Toul at the same time with a flush of red. For 20 minutes before dawn, there had been a queer ghostly light on the boulders, but now a soft glow bathed everything. To see the sun rise and flood the cloud sea with light was wonderful, and soon the sun blazed forth.

It was good to sit by the cairn and view so much beauty, but a cold breeze rose soon after dawn. After walking towards the Lairig we had a fine standing glissade for 80 feet of height in Coire Ruadh, so good that I went back to repeat it a dozen times. At 7.30 I left the Pools of Dee while Dad returned to Luibeg. I climbed 1000 feet to the top of the March Burn over unstable granite scree, but eventually saw sunlight catch the boulders at the top. I photographed the snow bridge and then strode to Cairn Lochan with its spectacular cliffs.

There followed a descent to the col where a wheatear sang, next a climb to the top above Coire an t-Sneachda, down again and up to Fiacaill a' Choire Chais, and then the dome of Cairn Gorm which I reached at 8.45. Trains puffed in and out of the fog in Speyside, where firs appeared ghostly through mist that evaporated quickly in the sun. The Tap o' Noth stuck out of fog, but a cloud sea covered even the highest peaks in the north-west Highlands.

I moved towards Ben Macdui and had delightful walking over the long grassy slopes of Feith Buidhe. Broad snow wreaths still lay and I saw a hen dotterel with vivid plumage. At Lochan Buidhe, with the snows of Braeriach mirrored in the water, I had a bathe. Splashing in at full length was cold, but after drying in the sun and walking again I felt absolutely fresh.

West from Cairn Toul, 18 March 1948

On a boulder field a cock snow buntings sang. I lay an hour, listening to it and falling asleep. When I woke, the sky to the north-west looked ominous and lightning flickered out of clouds over Ross. Moss campion bloomed, and on each big flowering clump a bumble bee worked, a yellow and black species with a vivid orange rear. I reached Ben Macdui at 12.15, and noticed Ben Nevis looming through dense haze. After last week's storm, fresh drifts a foot deep lay near Ben Macdui summit. Bob said four inches lay on Tuesday down to 3000 feet.

I came on a dotterel pair at five yards, the cock duller than the richly coloured hen. She continually chased the smaller cock and at the end of each rapid run stopped to fan her tail and raise her wings gracefully. Once or twice she crouched as if inviting coition, but the cock spent his time mock feeding. I walked down the Sron Riach, seeing two cock and one hen ptarmigan. A cuckoo sang at Preas nam Meirleach. I reached Luibeg at 2.15. This was my best day yet and I have always wished to walk the four tops. Not very tired tonight, I could have gone much further.

23 June. Bivouac in Gleann Einich
It was such a grand evening at Nethy Bridge that Dad and I decided to climb Braeriach, even though clouds touched the high Cairngorms. Leaving the car at the locked gate at Lochan Deo we had a fine walk up the wood in the dusk, with tawny owls hooting and a cuckoo singing. Braeriach looked impressive from Caigeann Beanaidh, with white cloud spilling over the plateau and into the corries. A bat flitted below the site of the Lower Bothy. Clouds blotted out the last pale blue sky and crept lower on Sgoran Dubh. We put on extra clothes, and after I made heather beds we slept half an hour. It became fairly dark at 1.15, the darkest of the night, and hurrying clouds down to 2000 feet filled the sky. We gave up the idea of climbing Braeriach.

Packing up, we walked the five miles in 70 minutes. The sky lightened as we reached the car, but heavy rain fell soon after. We slept 1½ hours in the car, and woke to see a clear sky. Feeling cold, we ran to the footbridge, a grand morning, with mist rising off the Cairngorms. It was dead calm. I have never experienced such utter silence. It drummed in my ears, and I could hear no other sound but the rushing of Am Beanaidh far off. We left Lochan Deo at 5 am to drive to Loch an Eilein and Loch Insh, looking for birds, and had a cup of tea at Pot Luck tearoom in Aviemore before driving home to Turriff.

30 June. Leaving school
At the prize-giving I won book tokens as prizes and then finally left Turriff Senior Secondary School. Afterwards, the entire 6th year class of Jean Gaul, Christine Imray and I celebrated our last day by going for a coffee at a bakery in Main Street, an exceptional treat. I packed for my holiday tonight, but the weather is bitter, more akin to October.

1 July. To Rothiemurchus
With a big load I cycled to Huntly, caught a train to Craigellachie, and then a slow train reaching Boat of Garten at 4. It rained all forenoon but then stopped, so I had a nice cycle run to Coylum. I continued up the path to camp near the River Druie. After a walk up the wood I brewed tea on my stove and then went into my sleeping bag after cutting bracken for a mattress. It is grand to be in Rothiemurchus again, especially on my first long camping trip. I heard roding woodcock call frequently in flight.

2 July. In Rothiemurchus
A gloomy day with showers. I slept like a Rothiemurchus log last night and woke at 8 to see a lovely grey wagtail outside as I opened the tent door. Later I cycled to Aviemore, next to the path cross-roads south of the Cairngorm Club footbridge, and then to Loch Morlich and down Glen More, looking for birds. I saw a twite on the moor and a greenshank at Lochan nan Geadas. In the evening I thought how nice it would be to have fresh milk, so I strode to Upper Tullochgrue, a dairy farm with prizes pinned on the doors. Mr Collie gave me a pint of creamy milk and we had a long chat about the hills. Tonight I prepared for going to Gaick.

3 July. To Gaick
Heavy rain overnight. As I ran to Upper Tullochgrue with the milk pail the sun blazed gloriously, fine to feel it after rainy days. I cycled off at 10.20, facing a strong head wind. Sedge warblers abounded at the Insh marsh. At noon I reached Kingussie, where I had an ice-cream and then cycled up Glen Tromie.

Beinn a' Ghlo from top of Cairn Toul, 18 March 1948

The road rolled mile after mile, and I thought I would never reach Gaick. In the lower glen, alder, birch and juniper run up to steep screes. Great numbers of willow warblers fed fledged young, and in open parts many wheatears. A twite fed a flying chick at a deserted croft, and the long grassy flat and junipers below Croidh-la held about 50 ring ouzels.

The glen's upper moor seemed dreary, accentuated by gloom as the sun vanished at 1. At Loch an t-Seilich dam, water roars into a four-mile tunnel to Loch Cuaich and Loch Ericht. A cock peregrine stooped at a small bird, so fast that the wind screamed through his wings.

At 2.30 after a 30-mile bike run I reached Gaick Lodge at 1450 feet. The hills are steep-sided, the glen floor flat, and the summits consist mostly of plateaux short of 3000 feet. Stalker Alick Sutherland stays in a cottage, usually alone, but just now has a sister-in-law up for the season. They made me at home at once. She gave us a plain tea at first, a high tea an hour later with four fried eggs and sausages, and later a supper of fresh salmon! Alick said a dipper had nested near the lodge. A raven pair and eagle pair have bred successfully and yesterday he saw a duck goosander with two big young on the loch. A peregrine nested this year, and he shot the hen and her fledged young.

After 5 o'clock it began to rain and fell in sheets into the night. A gale rose, and it would have been an appalling night to be out, even for a few minutes. The hills are so steep and catchments on the plateaux so big that the burns rise and fall quickly. A waterfall near the lodge was a roaring torrent and rose to that height within an hour.. Tonight I slept in a bothy with beds, mattresses and blankets – luxury.

4 July. At Gaick

I slept till Alick called me. The wind moved to north-west and rain fell as we left after breakfast on a long walk to an eyrie. Approaching the crag, we noticed the hen soaring high, watching us. The nest held two eaglets, one twice as big as the other, a larger difference than I have ever seen. While the big one walked about, the small one crouched bedraggled in a corner out of the rain. With a long tail, the big one could easily have flown if we had gone near. Alick said they hatched about 20–24 April. (In August he told me that the small one eventually flew).

We returned by a hilltop where a gale blew lashing rain, and saw a ptarmigan sheltering 10 chicks that could flutter. Back at the lodge, Alick's sister-in-law served a huge lunch and we could hardly move afterwards. It rained all afternoon, but after tea I walked to the plateau east of the lodge, where a bitter north gale blew, dry for once as I ran down the zigzag path to the lodge.

5 July. To the Lairig Ghru

Last night I was as cosy as could be wished. After breakfast, Alick said an estate lorry would give me a lift to Kingussie. While we waited, one of two young girl relatives of Alick's on holiday sang in Gaelic. Then I stood in the back of the lorry as it bumped down the road. I cycled from Kingussie to Aviemore, seeing wood warblers with fledged young near Loch Insh, and in a fir wood numerous redstarts with some beautiful cocks, and a brood being fed.

At Aviemore I sent my cycle home by rail and then walked to my camp above Coylum. I ran up to Upper Tullochgrue for two pints of milk and two eggs. After a meal I moved my tent up the wood, heavy going with a big pack. I thought of camping at the former Allt Dhru croft, but as soon as I sat down there, midges set upon me. Then I walked to the last trees, where I found a nice site on soft blaeberry, and after a brew of coffee went to bed at 11. Dusk had fallen and a great silence rivalling any I have yet experienced, broken only by the rushing burn below.

6 July. To Ben Macdui plateau and Luibeg

After a comfortable night I woke before 6 to a fine frosty morning. On the stove I made breakfast including fried eggs and yalla haddies (yellow smoked haddocks). While scraping the porridge pot I heard a queer rattling above. The trill came nearer, and eventually a crested tit sat on a twig five feet away, a perfect picture with its crest blowing in the breeze and loudly trilling in rivalry to my scraping.

At 7.30 I left, with the 10-lb tent in my hands, which cut the strain of the heavy pack. At the summit I turned up the March Burn, and a tiring climb followed on steep scree. I was glad to drop my load near Lochan Buidhe and erect the tent. Mist had come from the north-west and sleet swept the plateau, so I crawled inside and had a drum-up of cocoa. Then I covered everything inside in case of fresh snow, and weighed the tent all round with boulders.

In thick mist, sleet and a gale I left at 11 for Luibeg. With a light pack I felt almost like running, after carrying 70 lb. Despite the bad weather, a cock snow bunting sang loudly. As I reached the North Top, snow began to fall in big wet flakes. At the summit the wind had an icy lash and I hurried down the Sron Riach, arriving at Luibeg in heavy rain at 2.30. It was just like coming home to sit at the kitchen fire and drink tea. The rain stopped later and I went to Braemar on the back of Bob's motor bike. There I met Turriff schoolmate Calder and a pal on a cycling holiday. They looked thoroughly miserable and chilled in their shorts and thin shirts.

8 July. At Luibeg

Bitterly cold north gale with continuous heavy rain. I mended Bob's skis in the forenoon. We lit a big fire in the bothy with a cauldron of water to boil the skis and make the wood pliable. As the rain stopped in the afternoon, I ran up Sgor Dubh. An icy wind blew there and I ran down to Luibeg to arrive tingling all over. Soon after, the wind rose to a howling gale and clouds parted to show a pale blue patch between tall snow clouds. Many deer grazed low tonight. The firs groaned and shuddered in the blasts, and as I turned the house corner a gust almost blew me off my feet. I could not help thinking of my tent on the plateau and went to sleep with my mind not at ease.

14 July. Camp on Ben Macdui

A grand day at last, so I walked up the Lairig path with Bob, leaving my pack at the foot of Glen Geusachan. In roasting sun, Bob and I spent the day exploring cliffs in the glen and reached Corrour Bothy at 3, where we loafed a while and then parted. I found a good place to cross Dee further up, and then walked up Allt Clach nan Taillear. A cloud bank had formed to the north-west, and as I reached the head of the burn it hid the sun and swept the plateau.

Cairn Toul from Derry Cairngorm, 3 April 1948

At 4150 feet I came on a cock ptarmigan and four hens with broods, the young keeping with their respective mothers. As I reached the top, the mist cleared. For ten seconds I stood in glorious sun looking through a hole to Ben Lawers, but soon visibility fell to ten yards.

Near the North Top I found a dead shrew. I met two lost Englishmen who sought Aviemore, and showed them the route down to the Lairig. A lovely cock snow bunting sang from a boulder and an alarmed dotterel called. I had difficulty finding my tent and on going inside saw water three inches deep on my groundsheet and my blanket sopping, probably due to Monday's heavy rain forming pools in hollows.

After shifting the tent to a dry spot, I started my stove at 7 pm as sleet began to fall, and cooked a big meal. Then at 8.15 I crawled inside my sleeping bag, fortunately dry, and fell asleep at once.

15 July. Camp on Ben Macdui

Last night I slept well, except when I woke in pitch darkness about 2 am to hear scraping on the tent. Quickly I became alert. At first I imagined the spectre Am Fear Liath Mor looking in, but afterwards heard the clucking of a hen ptarmigan with small chicks, and then stillness. I had a comfortable night. The springy grass of the plateau makes a good mattress.

After waking at 9.30, I cooked porridge for breakfast. Packing up because of bad weather, I again became a mule. I had never been in such thick summer mist, with visibility five yards. Not a breath of wind stirred in the cold air, and I felt a thunderstorm might be brewing. The easy way out of the mist was down the March Burn to the Lairig, but I headed over Ben Macdui. I had gone only 100 yards when I came on last night's dotterel with three big chicks. A cock, he showed injury-feigning. A snow bunting sang and a black-headed gull stood in the mist. I took an hour to reach Ben Macdui, at times checking bearings every few yards. After coming out of mist above Lochan Uaine, I reached Luibeg at 2.30, grand to drop my 68-lb pack. Heavy rain fell tonight.

24 July. Carn Mor Dearg and Ben Nevis

After driving to Fort William we walked to Meall an t-Suidhe, seeing wheatears and a twite family. Gloomy mist fell to 3400 feet, but then cleared so we walked to Allt a' Mhuillin and up Carn Beag Dearg. The wind rose, on Carn Mor Dearg to gale force. The Ben Nevis cliff was the most impressive we have seen, its gullies filled with snow. We found the arete interesting, and tricky in the gale. Over Coire Leis a hen peregrine stooped and five ravens soared.

From the summit we saw no further than Buachaille Etive due to haze. For a minute we came into glorious sun, almost above the cloud. After looking at the cliffs we walked down the path. What a blot on such a fine hill to have a cart-track all the way. Today, out of 20 folk, not one looked as if he had been on a hill before. At the foot we sat in a burst of hot sun and reached the car after 4¼ hours up and two back. Hungrily we fell upon high tea in Fort William.

27 July. Aonach Eagach

On a lovely day, Dad and I went to Aonach Eagach. From Achtriochtan, we walked to the Study and then in a stiff pull to the ridge's east end at over 3000 feet, where we saw a fledged peregrine and the adult hen chasing two ravens. It took three hours to Sgor nam Fiannaidh at the west end, a magnificent walk. Airy all the way but never difficult, it gave a large vertical ascent and had great pinnacles. Although cloud swirled round Bidean nam Bian and swept low on Ben Nevis, we were in roasting sun all day.

The ridge gave superb views of Bidean nam Bian and the Mamore hills. On the Glen Coe road 2700 feet below, cars crawled like ants, and six ravens barked at Sgor nam Fiannaidh. From here a rough descent led to Loch Achtriochtan, bathed in hot sunshine in the floor of the glen.

In the evening we met MacCalum Cameron, who at 8.30 took us by motor boat to the middle of Loch Linnhe and round Eilean Balnagowan. The island had many birds including black guillemots and terns with young, 15–20 turnstones (half of them juveniles), and a juvenile grey plover. A flock of 25 greylag geese flew over, and we saw whales blowing. After sunset, Garbh Bheinn became a black silhouette and the waters of the loch turned dark except where they mirrored lighthouse flashes or rippled with orange light reflecting the sunset. We returned to Onich at 11 after a grand run.

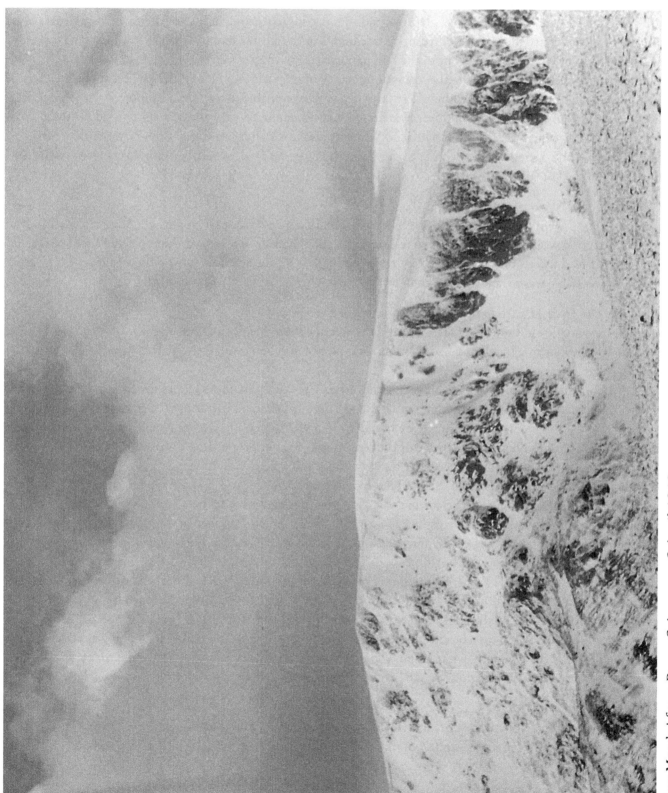

Ben Macdui from Derry Cairngorm, 3 April 1948

3 August. Beinn Eighe

Cold and dull this morning as Dad and I left Garve. By the time we reached Kinlochewe the sun shone and clouds drifted before a fresh wind. Leaving the car at Camasaig, we walked up a steep corrie with white quartzite scree to Sgurr nan Fhir Duibhe at over 3000 feet. From here the summit stood miles away, like a separate hill. Now we dropped and then climbed to the shapely cone of Sgurr Ban, then another drop and rise to Spidean Coire nan Clach, followed by another to Coinneach Mhor, a fine top on a mossy plateau. Along the ridge the views changed and Liathach looked inviting as we moved west. It is a magnificent hill, but Beinn Eighe IS hard to beat.

From a col beyond Coinneach Mhor we climbed to the attractive Ruadh Stac Mor at 3309 feet, a shapely nipple of white quartzite rising from a surrounding green flat. Breathtaking views opened to Lewis, over blue Loch Maree to An Teallach's tangled ridges and pinnacles, over glittering moorland lochs to square-cut Beinn Alligin, across the dark cliffs of Coire Mhic Fhearchair to the Skye Cuillin capped by clouds, south to Rum and many peaks towards Ben Nevis, and the vivid blue sea sparkling in sunshine, one of the best panoramas I have ever seen.

After basking in the sun and enjoying the marvellous clarity of the views for ¼ hour, we circled above the cliffs of Coire Mhic Fhearchair to Coinneach Mhor, where I found a hare leveret able to run. Over splintered screes we walked to Spidean and then down screes for 1000 feet. Reaching Loch Bharanaichd we walked on a hot road for three miles to the car, past lovely scenery at wooded Loch Clair. We came to the car after nearly eight hours, more than 16 miles, and 5000 feet of ascent. I spotted a golden eagle over Beinn Eighe as we drove to Garve, with lovely views of the hills plum-coloured in the last sun.

19 August. To the Shelter Stone

In the forenoon I went up Derry wood with Bob to help with a stag he shot last night. Then at 3.15 I left for the Shelter Stone in good weather and reached it at 6. Two Elgin chaps had already arrived. After a drum-up of cocoa and fried stag's liver I read the visitors' book. We went to bed at 8.30, as a cold north-west wind blew billowy clouds high above. The Garbh Uisge was a sight tonight, thundering down with great sheets of spray leaping off.

20 August. Over Ben Macdui to Corrour

Last night was my first at the Shelter Stone, comfortable despite rustling noises from a mouse. When we looked at our watches we saw 9.45 am. The mouse had eaten the best part of two buns and two tomatoes in the rucksack of one of the Elgin chaps. It must be a mountaineer!

At 12.15 I left in dull but clear weather, and climbed Castle Gates Gully, in places like a shower bath. The rock walls streamed with water. A waterfall came over one choke stone, and I had to stand in it for two seconds before scrambling on to the wall so as to surmount the stone. I reached the top at 1.15 after a loose wet climb, with even the biggest boulders insecure. After looking over the edge of the stupendous Shelter Stone Crag I walked to the Snowy Corrie, seeing some broad snow wreaths, and bigger ones between there and the Feith Buidhe.

As I reached Ben Macdui summit at 2.20, a blue hare ran near the cairn. I had a fine view, the Fife Lomonds, Lammermuirs and Ben Nevis being very clear, but thick weather prevailed to the north-west. As I left to descend scree into Glen Dee, fine sleet fell. I waded across Dee to Corrour Bothy, which I reached at 4.30. The floor had plenty of dry heather. After cooking soup, stag's liver, potatoes and cocoa, I read the visitors' book outside until midges became too annoying.

To escape I ran up the Devil's Point. By the time I reached the top the clouds had broken and a cold north-west wind swept snow clouds over Cairn Toul. I saw the sun sink over the edge of the Moine Mhor. A big stag with a great spread of antlers stood on the Buidheanach and trotted towards Loch nan Stuirteag as I came near. Back at the bothy I made cocoa and sat outside. It was a beautiful night, with the sun burning red on Ben Macdui, long after deep shade had come to Glen Dee. To the south, white clouds rode high against a velvety blue-grey sky, and a frosty mist formed over the river. I crawled into my sleeping bag at 9.30 and slept at once.

21 August. Corrour to Luibeg

I awoke at 9 am after a cosy night's rest, and when I opened the door from the fairly dark bothy I fell back, dazed by sudden brilliance. I went out into the finest morning I have ever seen. Frost gripped the ground and everywhere lay

Corrour Bothy below the Devil's Point, 5 April 1948

a deposit of hoar crystals almost an inch deep. The heather, delicately fretted with frost, sparkled in blazing sunshine. The air was still and it felt good to be alive. Not a cloud broke the sky, save a few flaming daggers above Ben Macdui, so I looked forward to a very fine day on the tops. After a splash in Allt a' Choire Odhair I cooked breakfast. By the time I had eaten, a cold wind had arisen, the sky filled with dark clouds racing from the south-east, and gloomy mist enveloped the tops. I had to drop any idea of going high, and left for Luibeg in rapidly worsening weather. The afternoon I spent helping Bob to saw logs. In the evening it was good to sit by a roaring fire, hearing the firs shuddering in the gale and rain lashing.

22 August. Ben Macdui

At 10.30 I left for Ben Macdui and reached the top at 12.45. Cold and blustery at first, it became wilder as I climbed, with a great wind buffeting me and almost knocking me down. The sun shone through holes in big white cumulonimbus clouds, but I encountered heavy sleet at the plateau and then wet hail driven by a wind of at least 60 mph. Mist engulfed the plateau and the roaring gale grew stronger, numbing my face. Half-soaked, I reached the cairn and sat shivering in its shelter while I got back my breath. Better was to come, for the sun burst through the clouds, which rapidly cleared off the summit, and I saw Aviemore and Braeriach. Then the clouds won again and flung hail over the plateau.

In thick mist I descended towards Loch Etchachan and came out of the mist as I crossed to Derry Cairngorm. There a hurricane blew, and freak blasts tore out gravel and plants, flinging them away in whirlwinds of fury. I had to crawl on hands and knees on the top, followed by a drenching of rain as I descended to Carn Crom. I reached Luibeg at 3.30, just in time, for soon after the rain lashed down torrentially for hours.

23 August. Leaving Luibeg

Sheets of rain in the forenoon. I left at 1 o'clock and walked to Braemar by 3.30. It was a fine walk, but I encountered an intense downpour at Corriemulzie, where rain fell so hard that water sprayed 3–4 feet above the road. Brilliant sunshine burst out afterwards, and in a strong wind I soon dried. Some magnificent white cauliflower clouds, a rain-washed blue in the sky, and the Cairngorms purple and brown made a fine picture. I took a bus to Aberdeen and another to Turriff. At Oldmeldrum, greyish-green rays rose into the sky opposite the setting sun.

29 August. To Drumochter

I decided to go to Dalwhinnie, as Dad would be driving to Dufftown on business. He went a few miles further to Craigellachie, where I caught a bus to Grantown and then a train to Dalwhinnie. Mist lay low and a strong wind swept heavy showers across the moor. I walked up the road to Drumochter Lodge, where I asked the gamekeeper if I might sleep in a shed. Though very friendly, he said better not, because the shooting toffs are up, but try at a railway carriage used by two men working the Balsporran signal box.

When I knocked there, Bob Sutherland and Davie Adams gave me a great welcome and ushered me into blessed warmth in Britain's highest railwaymen's bothy. After cooking a meal, we 'cracked' round the stove till late. Rain lashed outside and it was good to hear it from a warm bunk as trains thundered past.

30 August. Geal-charn of Drumochter

During the night, six trains thundered past a few yards away, but I heard only three. After cooking breakfast on the stove I left at 10 up the Coire Fhar path to climb hills west of the Drumochter pass. Past a group of cairns I walked on turf to Geal-charn and had good views of Loch Ericht before mist closed in. Arriving at the carriage at noon, I made lunch, and then how did the rain come down. A grand chap, Davie Adams has climbed all the surrounding hills. We cracked for hours till 11 pm.

31 August. At Drumochter

Last night I had a deep sleep, hearing only one of nine trains that passed. Low mist and heavy rain swept down the pass. Davie and I lay in our bunks until 10 and then made breakfast, finishing with coffee, his favourite drink. A pot bubbles on the stove day and night. He says the song *There's an awful lot of coffee in Brazil* should be *There's an awful lot of coffee in Balsporran*. In the afternoon I whizzed to Dalwhinnie on his brakeless bicycle to post letters. At Loch

AW sen skirts cornice on way up Cairn Toul, 9 April 1948

Ericht hotel I had tea while sheltering for an hour from torrential rain, and then cycled to Balsporran. At 7.30 the rain stopped and blue sky appeared. Soon the sun shone warmly on green Meall a' Chaorainn. It did my heart good to see such a grand evening at last.

1 September. On the Drumochter hills

Another wet misty day dawned, but I left for A' Mharconaich at 10.30. At 2000 feet I saw a roe, and Davie says there are usually three near the carriage, staying all the year round. A nice ridge leads to A' Mharconaich, and I reached the top at 11.40, with magnificent views of the Ben Alder hills, one of the wildest tracts of country I have ever seen. Rain and mist swept over them and they looked very attractive. Heavy rain now fell, so I descended by the Boar of Badenoch. A magnificent dog fox sprang from a bank four yards away to bound through heather, his long brush waving in the air, as good a view of a fox as anyone could wish, his coat a rich ruby-chestnut with a fine white-tipped brush. In pouring rain I arrived at the carriage and made lunch.

Later it cleared and I left for Meall a' Chaorainn at 3.30. A pack of 30 grouse chased by a peregrine passed with a rush of wings, the peregrine after them like a bullet towards Dalnaspidal. Torrential rain fell as I climbed Meall a' Chaorainn and dense mist came down. On springy moss and turf I strode to A' Bhuideanach Bheag, where the sun blazed through rents in the mist, with fog-bows and a Brocken spectre.

Now the mist lifted and the plateau became amazingly clear. Peat-hags stretched for miles. In fading evening light I hurried to Glas Mheall Mor and at the cairn sat long, looking at a wild view. Silvery clouds streamed like smoke off the cone of Schichallion, but mellow sunlight bathed the lower Atholl moors, with grape-blue cloud shadows moving over them. Sunset rays split through dark fire-tipped clouds over Beinn Udlamain, the wildest sunset I have seen. In a bitter gale I ran down to Glas Mheall Bheag, and after a jolting descent to Dalnaspidal I walked five miles along the road. At the summit I watched an eagle pair diving in mock fights.

I arrived at the carriage at 8, hungry after 18 miles and 4200 feet of ascent. Bob and Davie were out. After a meal I read a book. It is quite a thrill to see a train in the dark, belching out fire and smoke, and puffing hard to reach the summit.

2 September. At Drumochter

Heavy rain and low mist. We lay in our bunks till 10 and then made extended breakfast with cups of coffee running into lunch. In the afternoon I went on Davie's cycle to Dalwhinnie post office and back in pouring rain. We drummed up coffee when I returned and then had a good dinner. It turned out a fine night with lovely fleecy white clouds against a dark sky.

3 September. From Drumochter to Luibeg

Raining again this morning. At noon I said cheerio to Bob and Davie, after one of the pleasantest holidays ever, despite bad weather. I intended to walk to Dalwhinnie, catch a train at 2.30 to Aviemore, and walk to Clach Bharraig bothy before night. The first car stopped, a man going to Sutherland, and he dropped me at Aviemore at 1 o'clock. This was much earlier than I had expected, so after lunch at Pot Luck tearoom I decided to walk through the Lairig Ghru to Luibeg if possible and Corrour if not.

Leaving Aviemore at 1.45 I had a fine walk to Coylum, where the sun shone gloriously on the woods. After passing the iron bridge at 3, I walked to the last firs, a grand spot to look back over Rothiemurchus. This glen before the Lairig is among the best scenery in the Cairngorms.

A stiff pull followed to the summit at 5.45, for I had a heavy pack, but the evening sun was a grand sight on the red screes of the March Burn. A grey wagtail fed at the Pools of Dee. Now there came a long walk down Glen Dee, with magnificent views of the Garbh Choire in shade, although a sun-ray split the gloomy clouds to sparkle on the Lochan Uaine waterfall. Four snow patches lay in Garbh Choire Mor. Smoke rising from the Corrour Bothy chimney made me think of going there, but I continued round the shoulder of Carn a' Mhaim, where I staved off weariness by listening to crowing grouse cocks at dusk.

It was dark as I reached the footbridge at 8.30. How fine to come through the old firs and hear the burn rushing in the still night. The lights of Luibeg beckoned and I strode in at 9 to the surprise of Bob and Helen Scott. It was grand to drop my pack and be fortified by tea. Since midday I had eaten nothing but three bananas. I just touched a mattress and soon was in oblivion.

Friday 17 September. To Aberdeen
Off into Aberdeen today by bus from Braemar, after walking down from Luibeg. I saw my big glass lantern slides which the technician at the Zoology Department has made this week, on the suggestion of Prof. Wynne-Edwards. They are a grand set.

The annual conference of the Scottish Ornithologists' Club started tonight in Aberdeen at the lecture theatre in the Department of Natural History at Marischal College. Tonight, James Fisher lectured on the Birds of St Kilda, illustrated by some exciting slides. They were so attractive that they made you want to to jump off to St Kilda tomorrow! I spoke to James afterwards and we got on extremely well, almost as if we had known each other for years. He is very interested in the Birds of the Cairngorms, the subject of my lecture tomorrow, as well as sea birds, especially fulmars and we spoke long about the fulmars that I have been seeing on the cliffs of the north-east coast. James is intensely interested in the remarkable spread of the fulmar, and when I mentioned the various cliffs such as Troup and Pennan and Fowlsheugh, I was surprised how well he knew them and the history of birds breeding there, and how well he remembered the details of what I had seen in recent years. He was the most stimulating person I have met for years. I am staying for the weekend at W-E's house, along with visitors the veteran Scottish ornithologists Miss Baxter and Miss Rintoul, and James.

Saturday 18 September. At the Scottish Ornithologists' Club conference in Aberdeen
There were three talks at the SOC conference this forenoon. Harper Hall showed slides of gannets and peregrines in Canada, next my talk on the Birds of the Cairngorms, and then Robert Carrick on Starling Experiments last.

South from Cairn Toul, 9 April 1948

Before I spoke, James had sat with me in the front row and had encouraged me. Indeed, I got on so well with him last night and this morning that I found it good to look at him as I rose to speak and turned towards the audience. During the talk, I tended to look at him as if he were the sole audience, and I found this reassuring, while it was obvious that he did not find it disconcerting, for he often smiled. I did not find the lecturing so bad once I had got started – not a bit nervous – and though I could do no more than just touch the subject, still I said enough to evoke a lot of spirited discussion, especially about eagles. James Fisher joked at the expense of the SOC about the eagle census that he proposed but they rejected some time ago. Of course I had shown in my talk the value of a census in the Cairngorms and I was keen on James' idea for all of Scotland.

It was natural too that he asked the first questions, sitting in the front row as I stood at the lecture table. My answers quickly led to an excellent discussion between the two of us, but also induced a stimulating response from others replying to him and me, including W-E, Robert Carrick, and the Misses Baxter and Rintoul. After my talk, I sat beside James and we continued good discussion during the coffee break and later at lunch. My slides seemed to be appreciated too, so I was very glad, and I thanked the technician for his excellent work.

In the afternoon the Club went on a bus excursion up Deeside via Kinord and Davan. A dead short-eared owl lay on the road near Loch Kinord and two great-crested grebes swam on Loch Davan. We had tea at Torphins Sunshine Cafe and then to Aberdeen. In Torphins, Robert Carrick spoke well about his starling study and pointed out nest-boxes from the front of the bus as we passed. In Aberdeen, Ludwig Koch gave us a grand evening's entertainment with his recordings of bird songs and calls, after a dinner at the Athenaeum Restaurant. This Conference is certainly giving people an opportunity of meeting one another. Rintoul and Baxter in great form tonight at W-E's house.

Sunday 19 September. Conference of the Scottish Ornithologists' Club
The Club went out to Newburgh by bus today, a fine sunny day.

2 October. To the Moine Mhor and Cairn Toul
What better could one hope for? Bob roused me at 7.15 and a first glance revealed Carn Crom a soft velvety blue in a frosty half-light. Bob said, "Wakey, wakey. Get oot and up to Glen Feshie. It's a grand mornin." I rose in time to see the sun shine gloriously. First a streak of gold ran along the top of Beinn Bhreac, and quickly the flush of dawn crept down the slopes and fired the lower tops. It reached Sgor Dubh and burned gold on the red bark of the old firs.

At 8 I strode over frost-hoared grasses glistening in the sun, which now flooded the glen with a red light more vivid than I have ever seen. The walk up Glen Luibeg was grand, with coal tits in full song just like spring. It was good to be alive. From the new footbridge, Ben Macdui looked spectacular, with flaming red cliffs and screes against the soft blue sky.

I descended to cross Dee where the river rushes over granite slabs. Away at the back, grape-blue shadows etched the steep corries of Ben Macdui, and clouds still poured over Monadh Mor. Crossing near Poll an Eisg where an 8-lb salmon rested, I climbed on to Beinn Bhrotain by a broken cliff. Stags roared and a fine fox walked below the cliff. I climbed a gully with easy scrambling on sound rock, though other parts with wet moss and boulders proved tiring. The big crag to the south was a steep slab streaming with water. Not a breath of wind stirred. I climbed in shirt sleeves and still sweated. At the top, cold air rushed past and I rested for ¼ hour.

What a grand viewpoint this was, with the Geusachan Burn winding through green flats, the Devil's Point and its gullies in shade, and Cairn Toul buried in creamy clouds through which the summit jutted like a boat among waves. Cloud rolled from the west to vanish as soon as it reached Glen Dee. Eastwards, not a cloud broke the blue sky. Westwards lay a complete cloud barrier.

It grew cold, so I strode over rough ground to Beinn Bhrotain. On the last grassy slope I saw 45 stags and 30 golden plover. I reached the top at noon, stayed a short while, and then crossed rough boulders to the col above wild Coire Cath nam Fionn. Then I climbed to the plateau and walked over the Monadh Mor to Allt Luineag. Here I had lunch, a delightful spot. The burn rattled down, its water blue and sparkling in the sun. Green slopes rolled for miles, surrounded by whale-backed hills, the square top of Cairn Toul trailing silver cloud streamers, Braeriach's south top a warm brown, and the shoulders of Monadh Mor miles off in heat haze.

After dozing, I woke at 2 to the sound of geese and saw three greylags flying south 200 feet up. Suddenly I realised the wonderful peace of this place and a sense of being cut off from the world. Only six hours had passed since I left Luibeg, yet the folk I saw in the morning seemed remote. I might have climbed from Glen Feshie or materialised from nowhere. Everyday affairs seemed unimportant. It was most refreshing.

Rising, I strode past Loch nan Cnapan to Sgor Gaoith and back over delightfully smooth slopes. I saw 20 ptarmigan in fours and fives, already fast changing plumage. The afternoon had far gone when I began the long easy rise by Horseman's Corrie to the plateau. Fine weather still held to the east, but to the west a cloud barrier approached, engulfing Creag Meagaidh.

When I reached the 4149 feet top the wind became cold, and the sun hidden by hurrying clouds. I walked fast round Sgor an Lochain Uaine and Cairn Toul. Garbh Choire Mor looked utterly wild. Away at the back, two patches of hard snow remained, very small now. I estimated one at 50 feet long and ten feet broad, and the other circular one 25 feet in diameter and of greater depth. At the Buidheanach I raised 22 ptarmigan and two golden plover. Stags roared in Coire Odhar and I reached Corrour Bothy at 5 pm.

To my surprise I found Dad sitting outside. He had left later than me, come over Braeriach and Cairn Toul, and waited a while in the hope of meeting me. We stayed half an hour and read the visitors' book. Finally we left, waded across Dee, and reached Luibeg in the dark at 8 o'clock, a 12-hour round for me, almost 6000 feet of climbing and as good a day as ever I have had.

3 October. Derry Cairngorm

Bitter west wind and flying showers. I went up Derry Cairngorm in the forenoon, and in the firs saw a fine cock capercaillie and a flock of coal tits, some of them singing in the sun. I had a grand walk up Derry Cairngorm, where a gale blew hail showers. Three golden plover stood at the mossy springs north of Carn Crom. On the way down I had close views of 25–30 ptarmigan on the lee side of Little Cairngorm, sunning with eyes closed and wings spread.

Buachaille Etive Mor from Aonach Eagach, 27 July 1948

When I arrived at Luibeg, Bob had seen a tawny owl standing inside a window of Derry Lodge, so we went to free it. In fierce mood when we entered the room, it flew towards me, but I covered my head with a jacket and it swooped past into the next room. When we went there, it flew to the window, hitting the glass with its head and fluttering to the floor, dazed. Quickly I put the jacket over it and carried it outside the lodge, where my father photographed Bob and me with the owl, a bird of the beautiful orange-brown colour variety. Then I let it go, and it flew over 200 yards to settle in a tree. After seeing Mum and Dad off, we returned to Luibeg.

In the evening, Bob drove to Inverey on his motor-bike to collect milk, and I went as far as the Black Brig with him and then walked through the old wood. A hen golden eagle appeared and, drifting with the wind, met a cock in mid air, whereupon the pair flew out of sight. I wandered through the birches, now a haze of yellow and brown, to the top of the wood. Rowan trees were masses of flaring red foliage and berries, prominent against the dark green of firs. Four blackcock and three greyhens flew out, I saw a great tit, and robins sang. Returning downhill, I walked back to Luibeg by the glen floor on a perfect evening, one of the very best. The sun shone warmly, although snow clouds piled in great masses high above the summits. I had supper with Bob and Helen Scott, and then another fine evening round a peat fire. Sharp frost tonight.

4 October. Grouse shooting on Mar

Mist low and rain showers. Princess Arthur the Mar owner wanted a few grouse, so Bob, Willie Grant and I left for Meall an Lundain. We walked back and fore for miles, and Bob and Willie shot only one grouse and a Jack snipe, the latter on its own at a mossy pool. We did see about 20 grouse all told, but they rose far out. At Poll Bhat we sat to look at stags roaring from end to end of the Coire Gorm on Beinn Bhreac as well as among the trees. About 50 hinds grazed up Dubh Ghleann, so the stags did much challenging, although they have not started in real earnest yet. We arrived at Luibeg at 3 pm after a long tiring tramp, and soon shifted a fine meal of soup, venison and potatoes. In the evening, Bob and I went to the Black Corries to get another grouse, seeing only five very wild birds, but he shot one. We returned over Sgor Dubh and looked at Beinn a' Ghlo soft blue in the sunset light. Another sharp frost came tonight, and snow clouds.

5 October. Beinn Mheadhoin

After a long lie I set off at noon for Glen Derry. Below Craig Derry I stopped to watch rutting deer. A stag let forth tremendous roars, starting with a deep "ha-ha-ha-ha" and changing pitch as the roar rose to a climax. After a very interesting hour here I strode up Coire Etchachan to Loch Etchachan and then east to Beinn Mheadhoin where 25–30 ptarmigan flew past like snowflakes.

As I reached the broad ridge at 3600 feet, the sun blazed forth and shone gloriously for ¾ hour. I lay in the sunshine and dozed. Below, Loch Etchachan twinkled with studs of silver, and to the north, grey clouds passed in rollers down the green slopes of Cairn Lochan. The 3750-foot top gave a wonderful view of Loch Avon a vivid blue far below, and beyond it the sunlit Cairn Gorm and the Strath Nethy cliffs. What a grand high walk that is along the back of Beinn Mheadhoin, past fantastic 'barns' (tors). In the shadow of the great summit barn I was surprised to find an inch of fresh snow, and when I looked up I saw fog crystals more than an inch thick on the cairn. Several hollows in the rock held rainwater, with ice half an inch thick.

The sun now vanished as blue-grey cloud rolled over Ben Macdui and the air became bitterly cold. South I ran down to the triangular face above Coire Etchachan, seeing 20 ptarmigan. The cliffs at the top of the triangle are insecure, with much loose rock. Down rough slopes I ran to the top of Lairig an Laoigh pass and then walked quickly down Glen Derry. The stags were much more active, roaring, rounding up hinds, and driving other stags away. It was grand to come down through the old trees in the dark and hear stags roaring all over the hills.

7 October. Stalking in Glen Derry

Sharp frost, with banks of fog filling Glen Lui and rising as the sun strengthened. Bob, his brother Frank, Willie Grant and I went up Glen Derry, I riding a big golden-brown garron called Drambuie. On far and away the finest morning I have ever seen, the rich colours were astounding. Coal tits sang in the flock, two lovely cock siskins fed in a spruce, and a pair of flying ravens showed a glint of purple bloom on their feathers. Upper Glen Derry was glorious.

Near the old dam we spied for stags. Willie set off for a big one with 50 hinds and followers, and we watched through binoculars while he did a long careful stalk in their full view. A few of the hinds had come into season, but we saw no mating in 20 minutes. Most of the hinds saw Willie approaching and began to move away, but the stag took no notice, roaring and pawing the ground. Then suddenly he raced towards Willie, who fired. I have never seen Willie miss yet and he is one of the best shots in Scotland. The stag collapsed like an empty sack, dead instantaneously. Above him the hinds raced away. They had not gone 500 yards when a six-pointer descended from Coire an Lochain Uaine to claim them with a show of roaring. As he began to round them up, a heavy ten-pointer roared loudly from above, and tore down on the smaller beast. The latter fled at once, but collected a dozen hinds beside Allt an Lochain Uaine.

Now we crossed Derry Burn on horseback to where Willie had gralloched the stag. There we all ate our pieces and rested an hour, lying in glorious sunshine and watching stags and hinds up on the Glas Allt. These scattered trees on the Derry flats are magnificent, gnarled and shaped like huge mushrooms of green. All in all, the Derry is surely the most beautiful glen in the Cairngorms.

In the afternoon, Bob and I took the stag back to the lodge on Drambuie's back, and it topped 16½ stones when gralloched but not dressed. Frank and Willie took the other horse to Moine Bhealaidh. After work at the larder, Bob and I had a lazy afternoon, including half an hour's shooting practice with a .22 rifle at targets. It was almost dark when Frank and Willie brought in the last stag of the season, shot on Beinn a' Chaorainn close to the Inchrory march. Quickly we all skinned it, Frank and Willie drove down the road, and Bob and I walked to Luibeg.

This morning was the finest I have seen, and when we came over to Luibeg at 8 o'clock it was the finest evening I have seen except for that moonlit one last December in deep snow at Luibeg. A strange quiet lay over everything. The Derry Burn reflected the great firs in a silvery pool, while a frosty haze rose up the glen. A grey cloud hid Beinn Bhreac, and Carn a' Mhaim loomed high into clouds, looking higher than it does in daylight. A meteorite fell behind Monadh Mor. There was not a sound but the rush of the burn and the roaring of stags far up Glen Derry and high on Feith nan Sgor. Helen Scott served a meal fit for kings, a banquet with much venison. We spent the rest of the evening cracking round the kitchen fire, which gave off a grand smell of peat.

12 October. First day at Aberdeen University

On this opening day, students came to the university and received timetables. It was a lovely day, so I took a tram to Bridge of Don and walked to the mouth, seeing a duck goosander. Recently I have begun to think of making an expedition to Spitsbergen. In June I wrote about it to George Waterston, who told me to contact Brian Roberts of the Scott Polar Research Institute. I heard from him last week. Transport to Spitsbergen is easy, by coal boat from one of the northern Norwegian ports such as Tromsø, or sometimes from Oslo. Roberts says a seaworthy boat is essential if we are to do anything outside a small base area at Longyearbyen, because distances are great and weather "extremely unstable". Transport to Norway and then coal boat is expensive.

Pat Sellar is keen, provided our finances are enough. A big snag is that neither of us has any personal deep experience of boats in rough conditions. The boat should be the only main problem for us, but the cost of transport to Oslo and then from Oslo to or Tromsø if that's where the coal-ship departs, is going to be hefty, as is the expenditure on food. The equipment we should have already. Pat Sellar is dead keen if his finances don't run out. Perhaps Donald Emslie-Smith may go.

What pulls me away from this is W-E' s suggestion that if we decide to go instead to Arctic Canada, in which he's very interested of course, he would fix up a grant from the Arctic Institute of North America to cover our expenses! This seemed almost too incredible to be real, but of course he will know them and is going to Baffin Island with them next summer. It's good to know, though, that we'll be going somewhere anyway on an expedition to the far north. One trouble is that Canadian birds are largely taboo to us, I should think, compared with Arctic Europe, but many species are the same, and much of the literature on Eurasian tundra birds is highly relevant to North American tundra.

15 October. Bus to Ballater

Caught a bus from Aberdeen up to Ballater in the evening, meeting Mum, Dad and Stewart who went up yesterday to spend the weekend. What a difference there is in the air when you step off the bus at Ballater, compared with Aberdeen. I had a walk on the golf course later - a grand night with remarkable displays of aurora.

16 October. Ben Avon

A fine morning, hard frost and cloudless sky. After breakfast, Dad, Stewart and I set off for Loch Builg in the car on a perfect morning. Lochnagar looked grand and Deeside at its best. The run to Crathie and north towards Gairnshiel opened better scenery at every turn. Birches were a haze of yellow and brown, larches masses of feathery gold, and even heather was a subdued purple. Away at the back beyond wide-spreading fir woods, Lochnagar rose, its plateau dusted with a slight overnight fall of snow. From the last birches flew eight redwings, and many red grouse stood in the heather. We stopped at the top for a while. What a view, across the tremendous sweep of dun moor to Ben Avon, where the wind blew fresh and cold, straight over miles of peat moss, giving a wonderful feeling of vast open space.

Past Corndavon Lodge, the reedy lochans glowed dark blue in the sunlight, and from the first one rose an adult duck goldeneye to fly south-west, a lovely red-headed one. On the next lochan swam four ducks, a pair of mallard and – most surprising – two drake gadwall, their heads dusted with brown, slightly smaller than the drake mallard, and with a prominent white patch edged with black on each wing. Another surprise was to see three adult whooper swans swimming near the Loch Builg boathouse, startlingly white against the deep blue water. They seemed tired, and swam out towards the centre of the loch rather than fly.

Then we set off up boggy slopes, and near the top of Carn Dearg came quite close to a heavy stag near a hind and her calf. Nearby lay a young, very red stag with extraordinarily antelope-like antlers, almost like a goat. The big stag was royal in one horn but the other was deformed and only half the length. In the rough boggy ground south of Carn Dearg grazed 200 hinds with many calves, attended by some stags. The stags were doing much skirmishing and chasing, although only eight of the 25 stags had command of harems. At Allt Phouple an adult hen eagle flew close above us and beat along the steep grassy corrie to the west, where it raised many ptarmigan. It made a stoop at some deer but they took very little interest in this. One body of hinds and calves did, however, become more compact just after the stoop.

At 3000 feet we heard greylag geese calling and saw 18 flying south, about 2000 feet above us, and then turn to fly above the gap from Gairn to Quoich. Ptarmigan were numerous, about 40 altogether, most showing some white on their backs. We passed the first snow at 3500 feet and the freezing level at 3600 feet. At the Stuc Gharbh Mhor tors we stopped for a snack, and before we left it began to snow, very tiny snowflakes, although at the same time the sun beat down on one's face like a furnace.

We completed the round of the horseshoe and reached the top at 2.30, three hours from the loch. It was bitter there and the rocks hoary with rime and frost, so we did not stay long. There was an exciting view of the Slochd Mor, where the snow lay quite thickly. Westwards, snow showers obscured the central Cairngorms, but to the north-east everything was in sunshine and the houses of Tomintoul gleamed conspicuously. We saw across the Moray Firth to Caithness and Sutherland, past a fine view of the Banffshire hills.

Just after leaving we came upon 25 ptarmigan, and in two hours returned to the loch. At the car we were just having a welcome brew of tea when a fine eagle flew over, heading east. The ducks that we had seen on the lochans in the forenoon had gone, so we presumed they had been on migration. The run back put the finishing touches to the day when red evening light flooded the wide moors. From Crathie came a spectacular view, west to where the sun broke through wild coppery snow clouds. The Cairngorm Club had a meet at Ballater and I got a lift to Aberdeen on their bus.

3 November. Rock climbing at Cove

On a sunny afternoon I went to Cove with Robert Shepherd to attend a meet of the university Lairig Club. We did much scrambling on the cliff, and also climbing with ropes and abseiling, all quite simple. Routes varied from easy to severe, but even severe ones seemed easier because of sound dry rock, plentiful holds, and short cliffs with little exposure despite the nearness of the sea. We got a lift to Aberdeen in a lorry, which gave a thrilling ride at high speed.

6 November. Spey Bay

As I went in the bus from Aberdeen to Turriff, heavy snow and hail showers fell, and Tap o' Noth and the Buck of the Cabrach were white. After lunch we drove to Spey Bay in the car, arriving there at 3 o'clock. Dad and I then walked west along the shingle beach.

Waves were huge, with long-tailed ducks bobbing like corks and the wind straight from the north. From the lower

Spey rose 500 wigeon in flight, etched black against a lurid sunset which flared the river with an intense orange colour. Across the Moray Firth, the Sutherland hills held our attention, quite spotless to their bases. They shone a soft pink glow where sunlight rested on them, but deep blue in shadow. Snow showers trailed over them, and further north, Morven of Caithness loomed above a scarf of cloud, its summit cone heavily coated with snow. Ben Rinnes too was white from top to bottom. Off its summit ridge, drifting snow whirled high and caught the dying sunlight in flashes of gold. The clouds looked wild, like tremendous blue and red mountains edged with silver and gold streamers, and away to the north even the sea had a lurid gold colour, reflected from a huge snow cloud. On stony mud flats foraged 15–20 golden plovers and three turnstones, and amongst stunted broom bushes rose two reed buntings and four snow buntings. We had tea and then came home. Heavy sleet fell all evening so we had been lucky indeed.

10 November. Bennachie

In the afternoon I went to Bennachie with Bert Shepherd, bus to Oyne, a walk through autumn- tinted woods and then away up through scattered plantations and a sweeping moor to the final rocky cone of the Mither Tap. Visibility was very poor on a mild hazy day with no wind. Miles away towards Huntly we saw train smoke and could hear the train quite distinctly. What a black wild spreading hill this is, set in the centre of the farmlands! We hurried down in the dusk, running the last half mile to the public road, but missed the bus, after going up and down in two hours including 15 minutes on top. We got a lift on a lorry into Inverurie, now almost 6 pm. Ravenously we consumed pies, boarded the bus to Aberdeen, there had a fine meal at a tearoom, and spent the rest of the evening comatose before a fire.

17 November. Hill of Fare

I arranged to go to the Hill of Fare this Wednesday afternoon, Bert Shepherd, Sandy Watson, Henry Smith and myself. We just managed to catch the bus, no time to spare. The bus went out to Raemoir, and then we followed a path from a quarry up through bracken, heather and boggy ground to the west end of the horseshoe. At 800 feet rose three blue hares, one completely white, one still quite brownish-blue, and one intermediate. Farther up there were some more. It felt bleak and lonely up on the ridge, accentuated by the gloomy clouds, lurid dense haze, and quick approach of darkness.

Away to the east, a dark, tower-shaped stone building stood forbiddingly on the edge of the corrie, and over the moor a track led to it through groups of scrubby firs 8-10 ft high. We decided to explore the place, and the nearer we approached the more ghastly the building looked. Around it grew a few scraggy wind-blown spruces, shuddering in the cold wind. The door was locked, and there was an air of bleakness and dilapidation, like the ghastly buildings in old novels such as *Kidnapped*. We hurried down the track that we had now found, which should be good for skiing in snow, down and down into woods, not knowing exactly where we were going, and ended at the ruined Cluny Crichton Castle and eventually the main road. Within a few minutes, fortune provided a bus which whisked us to Torphins, where we fed at the Sunshine Cafe, before returning to Aberdeen by bus, entertained by Sandy's bothy ballads.

20 November. Meikle Corr Riabhach

A grand day, cold and dry with snow clouds. Dad phoned saying he was to go up Strath Don by car from Aberdeen, so I went too. We left at noon and had a fine run up. The countryside looked very colourful and the Loch of Skene was a lovely deep blue, with great numbers of duck and many swans. We drove to the Lecht, up over wine-coloured moors, past a grove of larches golden in the sunlight, on to the summit. To the west, Ben Avon was heavily covered with snow down to 3250 ft. When we came out of the car, not a breath of wind stirred. Then it approached, at first a mere whisper in the heather, then a pulsating blast swishing through the grass and singing in the wires of the boundary fence. We climbed easily on to Meikle Corr Riabhach, where a strong gale nearly blew us over, but it was invigorating. Sheltering behind the cairn to have a view, we saw miles and miles of hills plum-coloured in the sun, golden moors, and little fields and remote crofts in far glens.

To the west, fierce snow clouds obscured the Cairngorms, and as we turned to leave, the first snow flakes tore past, high overhead. We had scarcely begun to descend when a fearful storm broke. All we could do was run down beside the fence with eyes half closed, faces partly paralysed by driving sleet and hail. We tumbled into the car, breathless but happy. Now the wind rose to a full gale and I have never seen such a furious storm of sleet. After half an hour the sun shone again, and Ben Avon was visibly whiter. As the sun set behind it in a glory of fire-tipped clouds, the enormous snow plumes racing off the summit ridge were turned to flames. Westwards the pit of Loch Avon became black, as snow clouds pressed lower. For a second the last sun rays touched the top of a cloud above Ben Avon, and then they had gone as dusk fell.

We swung down into the glen, and in the first stubble field found a pack of 60 red grouse, three white hares, and a big flock of 150 snow buntings tinkling sweetly. A cup of tea at Colquhonnie, followed by half an hour in a snug cosy little lounge, completed the day. Dad dropped me at Mossat before driving to Turriff, and I caught a bus to Aberdeen. A drunk thought that I in climbing clothes and boots must be a joiner, greeting me with "this is the workers' bus". Incoherently he asked me to talk politics with him, but I got rid of him by falling asleep.

26 November. To Luibeg

During sports afternoon on Wednesday I went with Bert Shepherd to shoot at King's at the University Training Corps range, with .22 rifles. I scored 98/100.

On Friday evening I went up to Luibeg in the car with Mum and Dad. A stag very tame stood in the middle of the road at Inverey and would not budge, and at Glen Lui flats a herd of them could be picked out, their eyes flashing green in the headlights. Beyond Clais Fhearnaig a rabbit ran in front and became hypnotised by the lights. When I came out of the car it ran off the road into the darkness, but then returned, ignoring me and running straight towards the lights. As soon it came under the lights it crouched, and then, seeing me close, it tumbled into the ditch where it sprawled weakly. I had my hands on it but in a trice it slipped away and ran off uphill. I almost had my hands on it a few more times, but it seemed to be losing its attraction to the lights and increasing its concern about me, and the further away it went the faster it ran, an extraordinary piece of behaviour.

After arriving at Luibeg at about 9 o'clock, I cracked away with the Scotts till after midnight.

27 November. Ben Macdui

Dad and I left for Ben Macdui. It was amazingly mild, and we walked in shirt sleeves up the Sron Riach. The sun was very warm, and we came close to four ptarmigan that appeared almost dazzling in the sunshine and very conspicuous. One still retained a wide band of dark grey on the back and grey speckles on its head and neck. Very little snow lay, only a few cornices on Coire Sputan Dearg and some long streaks on Beinn Bhrotain, but Braeriach and Sgor an Lochain Uaine had much more, fair-sized cornices all the way along the cliff edges, and the gullies all filled too.

It was good to stride over the plateau and up by the Sappers' Hut to the top. A wonderful sense of space and emptiness is always gained in the last 100 yards to the cairn. Here it was cold, and we put on all our spare clothes and stayed up till it became too cold.

Leaving at 2 o'clock we descended Coire Clach nan Taillear where we saw flocks of 20 and eight ptarmigan and nearby a cock snow bunting. When we were half way down, some wonderful clouds blew in from the south-west on a strong wind. Barriers of creamy-white clouds rolled continuously over the Garbh Choire, and above us passed grey wispy clouds, disappearing over the top of the ridge in relief against a black sky. They had the most beautiful tails of whip and sickle shape.

On the ridge walk over Carn a' Mhaim we saw 30 snow buntings at one place. The sunset was very fine, a deep blue sky studded all over with silver-fired puffs of cloud. In the twilight, nothing could have seemed gloomier than Glen Geusachan opposite us, with the last pinpoints of light reflected from its bogs and the water on its sweeping black slabs. Darkness had fallen when we reached the new bridge over the Luibeg Burn, but a black Beinn Bhrotain was still outlined sharply against a pale orange-blue sky. Further down the glen we had a good view of the hill from the corner of the burn, with a beautifully symmetrical fir silhouetted in front. It was very still among the trees and the burn made wonderful music. We reached Luibeg at 5.30. Later there came a grand starry night with the wind sighing through the old firs.

12 December. To Luibeg and Loch Etchachan

I decided to go up to Luibeg for a short break before the exams, taking the last bus to Braemar. During a quick cycle journey in the dark, a very mild wind blew with heavy drizzle, but in places the full moon shone like a giant torch

Garbh Bheinn from Loch Linnhe at sunset, 27 July 1948

lighting the glen floor and the trees with ghostly light. I arrived as an unexpected wanderer and had a fine chat with Bob and Helen Scott.

Next morning, mist lay to 2000 feet as Bob and I left for Derry Cairngorm to shoot a brace of ptarmigan for sending to Princess Arthur of Connaught in London. Bob had a shotgun and I his .22 rifle. We saw a few, but with visibility at 8–10 yards we got none and I did not fire a shot. Several cocks still looked dark on the back, and we saw two hares, one white and one blue-grey. A howling wind battered us with heavy sleet, and dry snow above 3500 feet. On the north side, 20 ptarmigan stood on old snow but flew very wild.

We headed for Loch Etchachan, soaked. In a white-out, I took the lead with a compass. As we dropped to the loch, the gale eased and snow turned to sleet. Descent for two hundred feet often brings better conditions. Bob said "It's like coming to a different world". We arrived at Luibeg wet and hungry, and after a meal of venison we had a great crack while our clothes steamed at a fire.

14 December. Above Glen Derry

Away up Glen Derry I went with Bob to look for hinds, but we saw none within range. Above Poll Bhat, a stag had stuck in thick peat with his antlers pointing straight in from above. Body bent backwards over his arched neck, he flayed the peat with hind legs as we approached. Emaciated, he could not stand when we freed him, so Bob shot him. Torrential rain soaked us. After dusk I cycled to Braemar to catch the last bus to Aberdeen, with rain still pouring. The glen road was sopping and a severe storm burst, with rain falling almost horizontally in sheets.

21 December. To Luibeg

In the morning I went by bus from Turriff to Aberdeen and walked to the station to meet Tom Weir off a Glasgow train. In great form, he spoke of snow and more snow. After a snack, we shouldered our packs to two bus stations and finally boarded a bus that reached Braemar at dusk. A dusting of snow lay down to 2000 feet. In an icy dining room we had tea while awaiting a taxi to Derry. Tom enticed me with descriptions of Cape Wrath, and we had a great crack at Luibeg. It is grand to be here, and exams are already fading into oblivion. Prof Wynne-Edwards is here, going to Feshie tomorrow.

22 December. Moine Mhor and Cairn Toul

We rose at 6 at Luibeg on a perfect morning, with very hard frost and trailers of red flushing the sky before dawn. Thin ice lay in a water jug inside, and Tom and I, shivering, were astonished to see Wynne naked at the burn-side as he broke thick ice to plunge into a pool. We breakfasted early and it was good to be alive as we strode up the Lairig track and saw a lovely sunrise from the Carn a' Mhaim shoulder. As we rounded the corner, Cairn Toul leaped into view, warm red in the sun. Further round, the sun turned the snow-ringed crags of Coire Bhrochain crimson. We found it difficult to cross Dee on iced boulders, and I slipped, fell in water to the knees and scraped skin off a knee-cap and elbow. The sun crept down to flush the crags of Devil's Point a fine orange colour, and a scarf of mist floating near the crags became tinged with rose.

In Glen Geusachan a small flock of snow buntings flew about. We rounded the corner to face Sgor an Lochain Uaine, a fresh green in the warm sun, then up over frost-hoared grasses to frozen Lochan nan Stuirteag. At the col beyond, we entered a land of amazing beauty. The Moine Mhor sprawled into what seemed illimitable distance, a huge carpet heavily coated with hoar frost and rime, and sparkling with a satin sheen. Each grass blade, fretted with delicate frost crystals, shivered slightly and sparkled like diamonds. We had lunch in a hollow beside a snow drift and no more beautiful place could be imagined. The sun beat from a cloudless vivid blue sky with extraordinary heat for a December day, and not a breath of wind stirred. The silence of the Moine Mhor was deep, broken only by the cackling of ptarmigan calling on the swelling slopes of the Monadh Mor.

At last we parted, Wynne to walk to Kingussie and catch a train to a meeting in Pitlochry. Tom and I strolled north, realising that we were to have a memorable view. On Sgoran Dubh the sun etched each gully and crack with its own shadow, and wonderful warm light bathed the splintered cliffs. From the top of Coire Dhondail we watched cloud swirling over dark Loch Einich.

The further we climbed to the Braeriach plateau the more beautiful became the view. Over most of Scotland a cloud sea extended up to 2500 feet. To the south it shimmered with gold, while to the north-west a cold blue light pervaded over Ross. Every high hill rose crystal clear, deep grape-blue and splashed with snow, and we could see the Great Tower on Tower Ridge of Ben Nevis.

The plateau, streaked with hard snow, spread for an incredibly clear mile, and a round of Garbh Choire Mor revealed fine cornices throwing blue shadows into icy gullies. On to Sgor an Lochain Uaine we strolled in blazing sunlight. The sun had gone round the sky, still so bright and warm that we forgot the date and felt inclined to wait and feast our eyes on the richness of colour that pervaded the panorama. The cloud sea stood so high that occasionally clouds rose around a high peak and distorted its image. The Knoydart peaks seemed impregnable rock towers overhanging on all sides, and sometimes the clouds so distorted the Glen Shiel hills that they appeared as black cupolas and spheres balanced on top of spikes, and occasionally in mid air.

We left the top with regret and sped to Corrour Bothy. After wading Dee we walked home as the blood-red afterglow of sunset fired Ben Macdui and shot Cairn Toul's cornices with flaming gold sparkles. The walk through the old firs was the perfect finish to the best day of my life. In the perfectly still glen, there was a wonderful sense of peace in the chuckling of the Luibeg Burn flowing past iced boulders. We arrived at Luibeg at 5.30 after ten hours out and a grand day.

23 December. Ben Macdui

Tom and I rose early on another morning of hard frost. We carried skis up Glen Luibeg, a feast of colour in early morning light. Ben Macdui looked grand, flushed red in the glow of dawn, and the climb up the Sron Riach was a joy. Frost crystals glinted in the sun and threw blue shadows. The sight of a ptarmigan pure white against a vivid blue sky excited us.

Tom Weir skis on icy snow on Ben Macdui summit, 23 December 1948

From the edge of Coire an Lochain Uaine we looked down a long silver-lined cornice to glorious golden cloud-seas in the south, from which Beinn a' Ghlo thrust a spectacular prong. Many snow wreaths lay on the plateau, frozen hard. As soon as we tried to edge our skis, they would not bite, so we fell, and went off on sitting glissades. We had to be careful to avoid skinning and bruising ourselves on the rough icy surface.

At the top a vast panorama opened, with views even clearer than yesterday. The sun burned undimmed from a sky of vivid blue, and in every direction startlingly clear inky-blue peaks rose above a glistening cloud curtain. Ben Alder and Creag Meagaidh seemed close compared with far Ross and Argyll. Ben More Assynt stood clear and the summit ridges of Ben Hee topped the clouds. A billowing sea of blue cloud stretched across Caithness, the Moray Firth, and the lowlands, spreading like tongues into the Great Glen and the glens of Affric, Cannich and Strathfarrar.

Down in Speyside the cloud sea of yesterday had gone, but trees were ghostly white with rime. To the south and south-west the cloud sea gleamed golden in the sun, and I thought of the cities and people below in the fog. West of the top we walked to the edge of a steep corrie where we sensed great depth, looking to Cairn Toul and the Garbh Choire ringed with shimmering cornices.

Then we put on our skis and slid round some exciting fast traverses. The sun bathed the North Top a warm orange colour, chequered with hard blue snow wreaths. As we lingered at the summit for the last time, we saw the hills turn deeper blue as the sun dropped. At the slope east of the Sappers' Bothy we played for a time on quite a good run and then went to the top above Coire Sputan Dearg to await the sunset. A breathless quiet pervaded the plateau, and as the sun sank in a glory of red behind Ben Alder we saw a glow of warm crimson on the screes and snowfields. Silvery streaks on cornices rimmed Cairn Toul's inky blue corries, and the cloud sea beyond turned softest gold in the flush of sunset. Quite suddenly the sun had gone, the golden cloud barrier turned pale blue, and the moors looked cold in the fast-darkening light. We sped down the Sron Riach into the deep hush of the glen and a quick walk back to Luibeg.

With the Scotts away at a wedding, Tom and I had Luibeg to ourselves. After lighting a fire we made a meal and sat talking at the kitchen fire till 12.30.

25 December. Loch Avon and Ben Macdui

After a late start, Tom and I walked up Glen Derry. Glorious sun burst through at the top of the woods, with remarkable plum-coloured light on firs and heather. Some 200 hinds or calves grazed the west slope, where an eagle flew along the hillside, and in Coire Etchachan we saw a pair of ravens.

Clouds tore past Loch Etchachan, but through a hole in the cloud Ben Macdui appeared glistening with snow against a blue sky, looking very high. Silver clouds trailed over sun-shot Carn Etchachan, and as we walked over frost-hoared grasses the clouds racing past the sun had an edge lined with gold. Loch Avon now appeared below us, a wonderful contrast between the crags of Beinn Mheadhoin and the Sticil in the shade and the sun-bathed snowy cliffs by the Feith Buidhe opposite.

Lunching at the Shelter Stone, we found nobody had been there for some time. Then we climbed up the Feith Buidhe over spectacular frozen waterfalls and under cliffs with armouries of icicles 20 feet high. At 3500 feet we came on to the plateau, which carried an inch of rime. A bitter wind blew but the sun shone brightly, and wisps of thin cloud passing the sun became beautifully ethereal and silvery. Below on all sides, a sea of blue, creamy and purple clouds tossed and rolled in from the south-west.

It was a joy to climb to the North Top over snowfields hard as iron and covered thick with frost. Now and again, Braeriach appeared through swirling golden clouds. The Garbh Choire and the plateau behind it seemed magnified by thin mist, and from the top of Ben Macdui we looked over shifting golden clouds across to Ben Nevis, the only hill west of the Cairngorms that stood clear of cloud. A hazy gloom of orange cloud hid the peaks of Ross. Beinn a' Bhuird projected like a huge long log floating on water, with Lochnagar a little top above the cloud to the south-east. Silver clouds framed the Devil's Point and lay on Carn a' Mhaim. At the summit, two inches of rime sparkled in the sun, and we lazed a while, after coming up from Loch Avon in an hour.

When we reached the edge of Coire Sputan Dearg, swirling blue clouds filled the corrie and Glen Luibeg, the cone of Derry Cairngorm rose out of cloud, and a golden flush of sunset glowed on fog rime on the buttresses. Once an eagle flew round and caught the sun-rays in a flash of gold as it swung above 4000 feet. We descended fast into cloud and at 3500 feet came below it.

From Derry Cairngorm we had one of our finest Cairngorms views. The sun sank behind Beinn Bhrotain and at its last burst flashed with a pinprick of brilliant crimson for half a minute. We seemed to be on an islet above shifting blue seas of cloud, and on all sides rose wild hills shooting out of clouds. A tangle of ridges soared one after another to the west. Beinn a' Ghlo thrust its remote dome above the clouds.

The wind grew bitter. Down into dark mist we descended and came out of it on Carn Crom. Mist swirled round ghostly blue shoulders. Below, the glens lay gloomy under cloud. To Luibeg we came at 5.30, after eight hours on the hill and some fast walking on another great hill day.

26 December. Round the Dubh Ghleann

Frost and cloud seemed to portend snow but none fell, so we gave up hopes of skiing. Bob and I saw a raven this morning, and Tom, Dad and I flushed 40 snow buntings as we walked down the road to Clais Fhearnaig. Here a pair of eagles circled, and at the loch three mallard stood on the ice. After skating on the ice we descended into Glen Quoich. As clouds pressed lower, 15 blackcocks flew past and two roe deer stood in a sheltered hollow.

After lunch in the Dubh Ghleann we climbed to Poll Bhat, where we had grand fun sliding on black ice, running down the bank to attain a momentum that took us far across. As we came in mist to the outpost firs of Derry we had good views of a flock of 20 bullfinches with equal numbers of cocks and hens, a redwing and a fieldfare, and a hind with a calf and a stirk. The sun appeared through wild clouds for a moment. We returned to Luibeg for a good evening.

Chapter 7. Early 1949

3 January. Through the Lairig Ghru from Coylumbridge to Luibeg

In my diary I described this lone ski-tour on a stormy day of wind, deep snow and hard frost as 'by a long way the toughest and most exhausting day I've ever had'. I was, however elated to come through the centre of the Cairngorms on my own in deep winter, and learned much from the trip. I gave a full account of it and of the next perfect day up Glen Luibeg in my book *It's a fine day for the hill*.

24 January. Aberdeen.

Eric Hosking was here to lecture to the Aberdeen Branch of the Scottish Ornithologists' Club, and as Branch Secretary I met him at the train and had a good talk with him in the late afternoon. In the evening he gave a lecture to a large audience at the YMCA hall in Union Street, excellent slides of birds. Later on, Prof Wynne-Edwards took me along to Old Aberdeen as Eric was staying with him for the night. We had a fine talk, and then W-E took me in his car back to my lodgings in Broomhill Road at midnight.

11 February. To Aviemore

Prof Wynne-Edwards decided to loan me a pair of skis for a weekend with Tom Weir on Speyside, as mine are at Luibeg. From Marischal College he and I took the bus to his house in Old Aberdeen, where we had a snack and discussed ornithology. Then, carrying W-E's skis and sticks I took a bus back to Marischal for a physics lecture, next a bus to my digs in Broomhill Road where I got my kit ready, and then a bus to Union Street. In a great rush I ran down Bridge Street to the rail station all out, with a big pack on my back and carrying skis, sticks and ice-axe. I missed the Huntly train, having the frustration of seeing it steam out as I crossed the platform. I had bought a ticket earlier in the week, but in the rush this afternoon forgot to take money. The ticket collector asked in Scots where I was going and I replied in braid Scots. He lent me money to phone Turriff, and I told Dad I had missed the train to Huntly where he was to meet me. He drove to Aberdeen and I gave the collector his money back before we left. We headed for Speyside by Huntly, because snow blocked the Lecht.

After a meal in Aviemore we drove to Coylumbridge to see Tom at the bridge cottage. He is well looked after by Mrs Macdonald, a 78 year-old who is kindness itself. She said that news of my New Year trip, sleeping in the barn, skiing through the Lairig, and then sending a letter with a map for the address had "spread all over Coylum", and my kit is safe, ready for collecting. Tom says the hills have "bags of snow". After a long chat with Tom, Dad and I returned late to Aviemore.

12 February. Skiing on the Monadh Liath

A song thrush singing outside the window wakened me. Mist and falling snow veiled the Cairngorms and I noticed that gales had blown nearly all snow off the ridges. The drive to Coylumbridge revealed spectacular views of the Monadh Liath catching the sun and rising above great scarves of cloud. With Tom we drove to Newtonmore. Today the Monadh Liath looked more attractive than the Cairngorms, with far more snow, a lower snowline, and sunshine. Glen Banchor was lovely, the vivid blue river Calder winding through green haughs, the mellow red twigs of the birches, the spotless peaks glowing a soft gold colour in morning sunshine, and above them big silver-edged clouds throwing blue shadows on snowy slopes. In the glen's upper part, a-brown moor sweeps for miles up to wild rocky hills. We stopped the car at Glenballoch, an occupied croft with dilapidated sheds, some cows and hens round the house, and a few gale-blown trees.

Hail lashed as we ascended a waterlogged moor towards Creag Liath. A wild steep-sided glen leads to Glas Choire, and today the sparkling snow and cloud shadows racing over white slopes made it a place of beauty. From the snowline at 1500 feet we had a stiff pull on skins to the top at 2400 feet, with snow falling most of the time. A strong piercing wind met us, driving drift in our faces. Skiing into the gale, we were glad to reach a sheltered col to have food and a cup of tea.

The next slope rising towards Meall na Ceardaich had hard-packed powder all the way, and here in shelter the sun felt gloriously warm, but every summit trailed big snow plumes. Catching the sun, silver plumes streamed from the whole of the big corrie east of Carn Ban like steam from a huge boiling pot. On the plateau, conditions became severe, with clouds of heavy spindrift all the time, but it gave me a pleasant surprise to see that the Monadh Liath are a grand set of hills, for I had thought them dull. Today at their best, they gave fine vistas through to Drumochter, Ben Alder and Creag Meagaidh, where snow showers trailed like veils across spotlessly white hills.

For half a mile we skied fast on hard powder, then a lovely swoop into a deep corrie hanging above a rocky gorge, and a traverse for a mile slightly downhill. In late afternoon the sun had its last fling. Snow that lay dusted on the heather scintillated beautifully and the range of colour was beyond description. The twin rocky peaks of Spiorraid an t-Seilich looked very attractive, their cliffs a chocolate colour in the sun, a cornice along the top sparkling with silver, and deep blue sky at the back. We skied into the glen and walked to Glenballoch croft as sun gilded the tops. In the gale's aftermath, evening came with a quiet frosty hush, broken only by the noise of burns and a whisper of wind in the heather. After sundown the Monadh Liath turned cold blue across the dark moor.

At Aviemore it was a treat to toast our feet at the fire and tuck into a meal. Tom spent the evening with us. At midnight he cycled to Coylumbridge while Dad and I walked below Craigellachie. A full moon appeared and a cold hazy shimmer glazed the snows of Braeriach. What a grand day it has been.

26 February. Blizzard at Corrour Bothy and Luibeg

Tom, Dad and I rose at Luibeg at 7 to find there had been a thaw up to 3000 feet. A mild south-west wind blew rain clouds past the sun. Yet by the time we had breakfast the wind had veered west and wet snow fell. Walking up Glen Luibeg into a gale, we ran into a stinging snow shower and noticed that the snowline had dropped to 2000 feet. We appreciated a bonny spell with the sun sparkling on the blue water, and Ben Macdui soared, dusted with snow, beyond mellow light on the firs.

Shortly after, a blizzard came and visibility dropped to 100 yards. Huge moist snowflakes tore past almost

AW sits outside Corrour Bothy, 24 March 1949 (photo Tom Weir)

horizontally, with a gale battering us. Snow began to lie and dimly we saw the Devil's Point appear through squalls. We got wet while wading across Dee, for the water ran high with snow melt, but we carried a kettle, tea and some sticks, so lit a fire in Corrour Bothy and made tea. We dried our clothes and toasted our feet as hail pattered outside and on to the floor through holes in the roof. We were sorry to see the bothy in such a state, far worse than at Christmas.

When we went out, the sun blazed and the Devil's Point looked tremendous with a huge snow plume trailing off it like fire. Carrying skis up the Coire Odhar, we spent a few hours there, for the gale was too fierce to ski high up. Tom gave instruction as we skied on long tongues of powder snow lying on old snow. Snow fell and spindrift blew thickly, but it never bothered us, for the skiing engrossed us. We had another drum-up at Corrour after an enjoyable afternoon, and then waded across Dee to walk home. A snow bunting at the bothy and a dipper were the only birds. Bleak and cold the lower hills looked, under looming advancing dark clouds.

With the gale at our backs we had almost reached Luibeg when the blizzard came that we had expected all day, for the next hour the thickest prolonged snowstorm I have seen here. The snow visibly piled up. A brief lull came with a show of stars among wild clouds, and then the blizzard recommenced. Outside, the gale roared and walls of blinding drift seethed past with a loud hiss. Inside it was a treat, with a big fire and a good dinner including venison.

13 March. Storm on Carn Aosda

Dad and I woke at Braemar at 7 to find a dull morning with a west gale and snow flurries, and after breakfast a snowstorm. As we drove up we saw little, and in Glen Lui the snow drifted wildly. In a blizzard at the Black Brig we stopped to back the car with its radiator on the lee side. In a lull we continued to Derry Lodge, and skied to Luibeg in a blizzard driven by a strong gale. Already more than two inches had fallen.

At Luibeg we found Tom Weir eating breakfast. He had a grand time in Skye, and crossed the Cairngorms from Speyside on Friday. We went to ski as the sun came out, but the wind was too fierce to go high up and the hills trailed great snow plumes. We played on the hillock which gave a fast glorious run. At the bottom a bump rises near the burn. Here the skis were airborne for a second, a great feeling to shoot into the air and land with skis smacking a hard crust, and then follow with a run to the corner of the burn.

The sun shone brightly on spotless hills, but Dad was worried that the heavy drifting would block the road, so we left after an enjoyable time. He and I drove to Glenclunie Lodge, skied along the Baddoch, and then up the ridge towards Carn Aosda. Herds of deer blackened the Baddoch flats and a pack of 60 red grouse shot over our heads.

We had just reached the crest towards Carn Aosda when a wall of snow descended from Sgor Mor. Within a minute we were in the thickest blizzard I have experienced. I had seen a big rocky knob before the storm came and skied blind in its general direction, followed closely by Dad. As we reached it, the drift became so choking that we had to breathe through balaclavas. We gulped air in our mouths when drifting choked our nostrils. We could not see our feet, and drifted snow plastered us head to foot.

After ten minutes it abated and the sun glistened on the ridge. For a while we had good fast running near the knob and skied up to 2500 feet. Here the gale became severe and blew me over, while I nearly broke a stick in the fall. For two minutes it roared at tremendous strength, blowing Dad and me over several times. Deciding to leave, we shot towards the knob but a blizzard came before we reached it.

It came with extraordinary suddenness. One minute the sky was blue; the next the snow wall fell on us, thicker than ever. It lasted 20 minutes, so when it eased we left. Grand running followed to the ruined lodge. Then the skies cleared to show sunlit silvery hills, coal tits sang in the wood, and an oystercatcher piped on the grass.

24 March. With Tom Weir over Cairn Toul and Braeriach

Up early with the promise of a good day, we left Luibeg at 9, carrying fair packs as well as skis. Two ptarmigan flew across Sgor Dubh at 2000 feet and crows soared wildly. We made good time to Corrour Bothy, where the sun appeared and lit the white peak of Cairn Toul against a blue sky. Up Coire Odhar we walked to the snow, and then on skins up a broad snowfield into dense mist. We skied precariously along a cornice to the col, where the sun appeared and snowy Cairn Toul loomed above. Then mist rolled in again, but on the summit we came above it. Great barriers of cloud covered all hills except ours. Coire an t-Saighdeir was a scene of grandeur with silver clouds rolling into it, shimmering cornices, and furrowed snow slopes plunging down into grey cloud.

We carried skis in thick mist to Sgor an Lochain Uaine, when we stopped to decide whether to go on or return. Our heavy loads and the poor conditions tired us, but we continued by compass along the inner edge of the cornices. Avalanches had swept Garbh Choire Mor from end to end. On the plateau we skied on poor snow, wet and soggy. At the Wells of Dee a meadow pipit rose and a ptarmigan pair fed, the cock in summer plumage except for his head.

At the end of the plateau the skis slapped through slush and water as I led the way, but a faint blue sky appeared and, wonders, Braeriach suddenly rose ahead. What a joy to come out of mist and ski in bright warm sunshine. After hours in mist we noticed vivid colours, almost unreal. We slung off our loads and wandered, revelling in warmth and tremendous views. A flock of 30–40 snow buntings flew over, adding to our excitement, and Tom shouted "Great stuff"! Scarves of cloud hung below Sgor an Lochain Uaine and spun into the Garbh Choire. On every side, gleaming sun-shot cornices contrasted with dark blue snow in shade. Looking down Coire Bhrochain, we noticed two Cambridge students from Luibeg bothy starting a climb, and Tom wondered how they would fare, given such a late start.

Then came fast skiing downhill on frozen snow, and easy touring along Sron na Lairige, where Tom discovered he had lost his wallet containing £100. We had an exhilarating run down the Coire Gorm, very fast on frozen snow. In a last schuss we skied straight down at great speed, but Tom fell heavily in soft snow at the bottom. I swung past him, going all out, and finished by whirling down a long tongue of snow over the burn. At the end of my run, the hind ends of both skis fell through two feet in a piece of loose snow, but I had slackened my bindings. Tom had wrenched his ankle, so with this added to the lost wallet he looked more downhearted than I have ever seen him. Not even the wonderful peace of the evening could bring him out of it.

On the snowy ridges of Braeriach and Sgoran Dubh a salmon-pink glow lingered, while a few mackerel clouds shone with gold against the soft blue sky. All heavy clouds had gone, and after the sun sank it became frosty and calm. At 7 we reached the Lairig burn and then walked fast down the path into the darkness of the trees, tired with our heavy loads. Stumbling in the dark, we reached the road and saw the lights of houses at Coylumbridge, where we tumbled in at 9 pm at Mrs Macdonald's house after a tough day. Cups of tea followed and then bed beside a fine crackling fire. Tom's ankle began to turn stiff and sore soon after we reached Mrs Macdonald's.

25 March. To Ben Macdui plateau

A hard frost gripped the ground. Tom could not walk because of a sprained ankle. After breakfast I took his cycle to Loch Morlich. Under a cloudless sky the sun had great heat and shone with a hazy shimmer on the high snows. I cycled on a track by Allt Mor, walked up the wood and then in sweltering heat to Allt Creag an Leth-choin. I lunched at 3000 feet, basking in sun beside a snow bridge. The green meadow at the top gave a splendid view across to Sron na Lairige.

I skied up Miadan Creag an Leth-choin to Cairn Lochan. Surprised to see so much snow on the plateau, I had a fine run to the Feith Buidhe, now a great bowl of beautiful spring snow. The weather began to change very quickly as thunder clouds rolled over Braeriach. In a few minutes a thunder cloud began to build on Cairn Lochan and shortly engulfed the hillside. Visibility fell to ten yards and suddenly the air grew cold. Quickly I skied back over Cairn Lochan and at the Miadan came out of mist into warm sun. Surprised to hear yelping geese, I looked up to see 20 greylags fly north along the east escarpment above Lairig Ghru.

From the meadow at the top, a broad snow wreath covered Allt Creag an Leth-choin for over a mile, and on fast spring snow the run was a joy. In the middle came a steep part where I went straight, and then swung from side to side on the last few hundred yards. Then I walked down to the wood, where I saw a pair of crested tits. As I cycled down Glen More a goosander pair landed on Loch Morlich. Thick haze almost obscured the high hills and a thunder cloud towered above Cairn Lochan. I spun down on Tom's cycle, ready for a good dinner from Mrs Macdonald.

Low cloud and drizzle came next day, while a recovering Tom walked with me for five miles towards Loch Pityoulish and to Aviemore return. In the evening, Dad turned up in a new car. Tom was worried about his wallet, so I decided to go through to Luibeg tomorrow to look for it.

27 March. Twice in a day through the Lairig Ghru for Tom Weir's wallet

At Coylum, Mrs Macdonald wakened me at 6.15 and I ate breakfast in the bedroom while Tom chuckled under the blankets. I left at 7, travelling very light, and took Tom's cycle up to the path junction beyond the iron footbridge.

What a morning it was, with a crackling frost, a cloudless sky, and the hills brilliant and hard-edged! Coal tits and mistle thrushes sang and at Allt Dhru clearing a pair of goosanders flew low, chattering harshly and gleaming in the sun. I could have lingered here, but had to move and left the bike at the path junction at 7.45.

The next stretch up the wood was a delight. Sgoran Dubh looked most attractive, with the ridge past Sgor Gaoith spotless with snow, which gleamed a soft creamy colour and in sharp contrast to the blue sky beyond. With the wood in front it made a lovely picture. On the moor I made good time, because frost had hardened the peat and turned the snow hard and gritty.

At the summit I came across many ptarmigan, nearly all in pairs. Very excited, they displayed and the hens cooed, a high pitched note almost like a dog's howl that echoed across the pass, a most extraordinary sound. With drooped wings and fanned tails the cocks chased hens, and I saw one cock in full breeding plumage apart from some white on his head and neck.

A dusting of snow lay here. Heavy snow had fallen on the high hills, with Beinn Bhrotain spotless to 3000 feet. A pair of eagles circled Glen Dee. The hills looked their best, hard and sharp. From the Glen Luibeg footbridge Ben Macdui was spectacular, under much new snow.

Tom thought the wallet would be under a big tree by the bridge, but it was not. Carrying on to find if Bob had heard any word, I reached Luibeg at noon, five hours from Coylumbridge, including 20 minutes searching near the footbridge in Glen Luibeg. It was fine to be in the glen again, looking as bonny as I have ever seen it. Mrs Scott had a cup of tea in my hands before I sat down, and treated Bob and me to a fine dinner. They had no word of the wallet. After a rest I left at 1.30 with Bob, who came as far as the bridge. Seeing this part after Speyside convinces me of Mar's better scenery. A purple bloom glowed on the hills almost like heather bloom in September. The blue of the burn, green of the trees and snow-capped hills made a beautiful scene.

Later, from the Lairig path I saw a man standing outside Corrour Bothy. Thinking there might still be a slender chance of finding the wallet I waded across Dee and walked to the bothy. An Aberdeen hill-walker, he said "Where are you making for?" I said "I'm hunting for a wallet". His face lit up as he asked "Is it by any chance a Glasgow bloke named Weir?" He gave me the wallet and said he had found it at 1 am on Friday morning, on the path two yards from the bridge, where he stumbled on it in the dark.

Elated now, I strode merrily on, but it seemed a long pull up to the Pools of Dee, and I had much wading through soft snow where the sun had softened it. The views all around were wonderful though, especially of the Garbh Choire with its sunlit cornices, and Coire Bhrochain a place of delicate colourings where gold patches and deep blue shadowed gullies and buttresses made a fine contrast. After heavy wading in snow near the Pools of Dee, I was glad to reach the Lairig summit and sit for a short time, to rest muscles now a bit stiff with fast walking and wading for so long. The warm evening light burned on the March Burn screes, and from the summit I could see Rothiemurchus, Ben Wyvis and more distant hills of a soft blue colour into Sutherland.

Now came a quick walk down to the wood, as delicate colours flooded the hills, with fine plum colour on the crest of Creag an Leth-choin and rich gold on Braeriach's snows. I reached the path junction at 6.30 and spun down on the bicycle to the footbridge, where I saw a crested tit. From Whitewell, Rothiemurchus seemed like a great carpet, tonight especially beautiful because the low sun picked out each tree with its own shadow. There was utter calm, and not a sound but the rush of water in Am Beanaidh, and a mistle thrush and blackbird singing.

I hurtled down to Coylum at 7.30 after a tough day with 3700 feet of climbing, four miles of cycling and 29 of rough walking. It had been a grand day and Tom chortled when I produced his wallet. Ravenous, I polished off a first-class meal of Mrs Macdonald's.

28 March. Glen More

As I awoke, I said to Tom in the double bed, "I slept like a dead man last night", to which he replied "I've never seen a dead man kick so hard". A hot sunny morning greeted us. Dad drove to Loch Morlich and we carried skis past Clach Bharraig bothy, but Tom decided he should rest his ankle and I felt a bit tired after yesterday's long walk, so we returned after what Tom described as "the best ski-run we never had". After tea in Aviemore we drove to Loch Insh where 20 whooper swans fed in the shallows.

AW stands near the cornice of Coire Bhrochain, 24 March 1949 (photo Tom Weir)

29 March. A' Mharconaich

A grand sunny morning, and bird song was at a peak. Dad picked us up at Coylum, and at Aviemore station we saw Tom off on the train to Perth at 10. As it pulled out, he leaned out of the window to face us with a grin from ear to ear, and held it until the train vanished.

Dad and I drove to Drumochter and walked up A' Mharconaich, carrying heavy skis in great heat. Ben Alder lay deep under fresh snow and smoke from heather fires rose high. From the top of A' Mharconaich, a fast run led on spring snow for a ¼ mile, at first down a cornice and round a corner. Then came a half mile of a steep slope on a series of broad drifts connected at their corners, including a fast run straight down where the momentum at the foot sent me on the skis ten yards into the heather.

Near the rail cottages we drummed up tea on a stove by the car. A rail worker who lived in one cottage remembered me staying in the carriage with the signalmen last autumn. As Dad and I left in the car, evening sunlight flooded the hills, turning the heathery slopes to an extraordinary warm chocolate colour. These are great hills, fascinating in their starkness.

30 March. Creag Meagaidh

With the heat wave showing no sign of breaking, we left for Creag Meagaidh. Views became ever more attractive as we drove west, with the climax at the end of Loch Laggan where a superb scene burst on us as we rounded a rocky corner. For miles ahead, the loch lay as unruffled as a glass mirror, reflecting every detail of surrounding woods and peaks. Behind on the right, the snow-splashed Creag Meagaidh rose high, with Coire Ardair's cornices glittering silvery and the snowy broad ridge to Carn Liath glowing a warm creamy-orange colour in hazy sunlight. Around the loch, spruces and birches were reflected in the bay before us, with the fairy-like Ardverikie castle on the south side, the shapely cone of Binnein Shios behind, and further back a snowy Geal Charn softly blurred in the humid atmosphere. A blackbird sang and oystercatchers piped loudly. We could have stayed long here but Creag Meagaidh beckoned.

Leaving the car at Aberarder, a farm surrounded by wind-swept larches, we climbed the shoulder of Sron a' Choire. A corniced ridge swept to a cone above Puist Coire Ardair, giving wonderful views of the huge cliffs of Coire Ardair, sparkling with festoons of ice and snow. Alpine views surrounded us, for just to the south plunged the deep Coire Choille-rais, its cliffs heavily corniced and its buttresses smoothed out with furrowed snow. Further south-west stood the great east face of Beinn a' Chaorainn, a huge long corrie with cliffs thickly plastered by snow below broad shining cornices. Ahead of us, the plateau of Creag Meagaidh rose in a shimmering white wave, absolutely immaculate. For almost two miles we walked across its unbroken surface with the sun blazing and intense glare off the snow. The final rise along a corniced ridge was a joy, on powder snow lying upon a deep frozen layer, and with broken cliffs dropping to the remote Lochan Uaine to the north. We wished we had taken our skis.

Three hours from Aberarder we reached the summit, where thick haze obscured distant views. Soon after leaving we had a fine short glissade. Sitting on gas capes, we whirled down, sending powder snow flying. Then we circled the cliffs and walked down snow slopes to the Uinneag or Window, where I had a sitting glissade for 400 feet on wet snow. In Coire Ardair a big avalanche had come down a gully below impressive cliffs soaring well over 1000 feet, one of the finest corries I have ever seen. A raven barked as it soared effortlessly on air currents above the icy cliffs.

By the time we reached the birch woods in the lower glen, thin cloud veiled the sun. Coire Ardair looked fierce, its huge buttresses inky-blue and lit by shafts of sun. On Loch Laggan beach I made a fire of driftwood and drummed up tea. The smell of burning wood, the smoke coiling in still air, and a cup of hot tea by the loch made a fine end to a grand spring day.

31 March. Beinn a' Chaorainn of Spean

Again after a great morning, at the end of Loch Laggan we had a view that beat yesterday's for loveliness. Today the peaks were hazier but had a softness that seemed more appealing. Two cormorants swam in the creek and swallowed small fish, and two blackcock rose at the roadside. The view of Creag Meagaidh's shoulder looming between tall spruces at Moy Lodge was grand, and Beinn a' Chaorainn's east corrie soared above us.

Sweating in great heat to the plateau, we saw no further than Ben Alder because of haze. Enormous cornices prevented us coming to the edge of the east corrie, but the centre top gave a good view of one part of the corrie, laced with huge broad cornices, a most impressive place.

Swiftly we descended, running down a snowfield. A hare bolted, still quite white. At 2000 feet we saw ptarmigan, and on the lower slopes many pools with spawning frogs. At Loch Laggan Hotel we ordered a pot of tea, which we drank to the last drop. At Newtonmore I sent my skis by rail to Aviemore for collection in April, and then went to the signal box to chat with Bob Sutherland. He was at Balsporran rail carriage last autumn when I stayed there.

7 April. To Loch Monar in snow

At Turriff I rose to catch the early train to Inveramsay junction, where I joined a train to Inverness. Snow lay near the railway at Gartly and the sky was full of it, driven by a slight north-east wind. At Elgin it lay and fell heavily, but we left it behind at Nairn, though wet snow fell in Inverness. There I took a bus, seeing many duck on Beauly Firth. A search in Beauly gained me lunch but neither bicycle nor food, for all shops had closed.

I got a lift to Struy past foaming waterfalls and through tall spruces festooned with snow. I walked up the glen road for eight miles without seeing a vehicle. Cannich and Affric are the accessible glens because of hydro-electric schemes. The snow kept off although it was a dismal dark day with wet snow lying. Magnificent birch and fir woods grow in the lower glen, where I saw many redpolls, a few pairs of hooded crows and several crossbills.

Towards Loch Beannacharan a blizzard came on and I was thankful to go into a lumber-men's hut and stand at the fire. They worked for a timber company and most hailed from Aberdeenshire, so we spoke broad Scots. When they heard I came from Turriff, one offered to take me up in his lorry. Clambering in, we drove through a mass of mud on to the road. What a journey on the worst road imaginable! I got used to leaving the seat and hitting the roof. A blizzard howled and storm-lashed Glen Strathfarrar looked the wildest and most beautiful glen I have ever seen, especially the gorge, where a flock of redwings flew off. The driver took me nine miles to Monar Lodge. When I said I would send fags, he replied "Na, na, I dinna smoke and I dinna need onything. It's a coorse nicht and onywey it's nae my petrol I'm usin. It's the Jews' petrol" (a Scots Jewish family ran the company).

At Monar I met stalker Mr Fleming, about to leave for Struy in his car. I told him Tom Weir had suggested I call, and he remembered him well. Mrs Fleming made me feel at home with tea, scones, jam and crowdie, and then said "I'll show you your quarters", a house near the lodge. There I lit a big fire, my wet clothes steamed, and I cooked a meal on the fire. Upstairs I had blankets, a bunk, pillow, blankets, and - luxury - a paraffin lamp. Outside, wet snow fell.

8 April. A stormy day on the Monar hills

I had a comfortable night, and only once wakened, on hearing tawny owls bickering. When I rose at 8, snow fell thickly and three inches lay. I ran down to Loch Monar and will never forget the view as I came out of the wood. In front stretched Loch Monar, a cold blue with choppy waves, and at the back Maoile Lunndaidh a beautiful rosy-gold colour in the sunlight, deep under snow. To the left soared Bidean an Eoin Dearg, a sharp graceful peak. All around stood steep crags laced with snow, and far back, massive snow-clouds piling on a north-westerly wind. Beinn na Muice above the lodge rose steeply to a thin wedge that trailed a high snow plume.

I cooked breakfast on a roaring fire. Snow still fell. While collecting firewood, I saw Sgurr na Lapaich to the south glistening in a brief sunny blink, a great sight. Robins, a blackbird, a dunnock and a dipper sang. Planted firs and larches shelter the lodge at 700 feet, along with spruces, rhododendrons, ivy and evergreen bushes. After lunch I wrote a letter home. Mr Fleming showed me his hydro-electric scheme, working from a wheel on the burn.

Then I climbed Beinn na Muice. Occasionally the sun shone but clouds loomed with a strong bitter wind and frequent thick snowstorms. A wild view opened to the western peaks with the sun on them, black clouds behind and the loch surrounded by snowy slopes, and a fine view of Sgurr na Muice and Sgurr na Fearstaig blurred by heavy drifting. I had a slippery descent, plunging through deep drifts and cutting steps on iced rocks.

Because the shops had been closed in Beauly I had meagre food. Just as I remembered this, Mr Fleming came with a container full of potatoes and six salted herring which I put in the burn to remove the salt. I had a long chat with him in the afternoon. As a pair of eagles circled above the house, he said "They're fairly common and I've seen five or six together. As soon as my wife and I build up a stock of hens the number begins to diminish, because wild cats take them during the day". In the evening I ate a good meal of herrings and potatoes, and Mrs Fleming came with two pints of milk. A blizzard set in and it became gloomy, but I had a big fire going.

9 April. Glen Strathfarrar to Rothiemurchus

Last night a pair of tawny owls kept bickering outside my window and wakened me a few times, and then I heard spruces shuddering outside and a wild wind battering the house. Occasionally the moon, now nearly full, appeared between wild clouds and flooded the room.

When I rose at 7.30, snow still fell thickly. I ran to Loch Monar but heavy cloud and snow hid the hills. A raven flew over and a pair of mallard. After breakfast I decided to leave because of the bad weather. Yesterday on Beinn na Muice was trying because of the mighty wind, deep snow, iced rocks and thick blizzards. Solo climbing higher on these wild peaks in such storms seemed an undue risk. I decided to go to the Cairngorms, hoping for better weather to the east, because the winds had come from north-west. I had been unlucky not to have even part of a day of good weather, but regretted leaving such an interesting beautiful place.

Mrs Fleming told me a lorry usually left the lumber camp at noon, so I packed up hurriedly and left at 10. I walked fast through heavy snow, already turning wet. Wild snowstorms swept the gorge. At Braulen the keeper asked me in for tea, and I would have liked to accept his kind offer, but I said I hoped to catch the lorry, so he wished me good luck.

Wheatears had arrived in fair numbers and already some cocks sang. After Braulen the snow stopped falling and sunny blinks appeared. A fine peak, Sgurr na Lapaich formed a prong with a graceful centre top, snowy and glistening. Sgurr a' Choire Ghlais was spotless. What a grand loch Loch a' Mhuillidh is, with old firs along the edge and on the island! Here a duck goosander flew about croaking and a buzzard circled over the firs, chased by hooded crows. I could have lingered long here with the sun shining warmly among the firs.

After nine miles I reached the camp at 12.30 but the lorry had left. The lumber-men plied me with cups of tea and thick sandwiches of white bread and jam, while asking about Turriff folk. I left at 1.30 and at Deanie Lodge among old firs saw a few siskins and many redpolls. Three miles beyond, a man in a car passed, and – wonders – stopped to give me a lift to Beauly. He knows Desmond Nethersole-Thompson and likes watching birds.

From Beauly I took a bus to Inverness, where I had tea and caught a train for Aviemore. The train above Culloden Moor gave an impressive view. Ben Wyvis rose spotless under snow down to 2000 feet, and the Fannich and Monar peaks lay pale grey under heavy cloud and snowstorms, but the cone of Sgurr a' Choire Ghlais thrust clear, a triangle of shining white. As I stood at the window, looking over the blue haze of flat lands round Inverness to the ring of snowy peaks, some sunlit and others dark under snow clouds, I vowed to return. These peaks fascinated.

Evening sun glowed on the Findhorn moors. South of Slochd I saw that the Cairngorms had far less snow than the peaks I had left. Most ground above 3000 feet had a grey tinge, due to boulders projecting above the snow following severe drifting, so skiing would be impossible except in sheltered corries. Snow whitened the low slopes because of less drifting.

I collected bicycle and skis at Aviemore and cycled to Whitewell. Golden sunlight flooded the snows. Desmond Nethersole-Thompson was at a meeting in Aviemore, but Carrie gave me tea and sandwiches. I spent a fine evening with the family, and Brock played an accordion. They had no shed but Brock left at 9 to show me one at Achnagoichan, where I made a fire and cut a dry heather bed. As I turned in at 10, I noticed a white ring round the moon and a rising wind.

10 April. The Lairig Ghru

Last night the wind rose to a gale and heavy hail battered the corrugated iron roof, preventing sleep. I rose at 6.30 on a bitter morning with a cutting gale and the tops under heavy cloud. After breakfast I walked to Carrie's house where I left most of my equipment and cycle, but carried my skis, ice-axe, spare clothes and food.

As I left at 8 I saw two blackcocks and mistle thrushes singing, and among the last trees four crested tits. Above 1000 feet, three inches of snow lay, not enough to ski, but enough to make walking difficult. A trying journey followed to the top, where deep soft snow among boulders gave tricky going. Towards the top, snow fell and the gale became a near hurricane. I struggled carrying a big pack and skis in the face of a snowstorm. The gale caught the skis violently and at times nearly blew me off my feet. My face felt stiff with cold, and I was glad to see the summit cairn and sit by it in a drift. Snow fell heavily, gradually turning wet.

I put on skis at the Pools of Dee and ploughed past them in poor snow, though easier than walking. On the other side the snow slope ended, but the gale eased and snow stopped falling. Some heavy wading in soft snow followed.

Suddenly I would go in to the waist with one leg, and sprawl with my heavy load. Between the Pools and Carn a' Mhaim I made slow going and felt tired, though not enough to require an overnight stop at Corrour Bothy. With relief I saw a snow slope from Carn a' Mhaim to the footbridge, which gave a good ski-run.

I left my skis at the bridge and reached Luibeg at 4.30 after a tough day, one of the hardest I have ever had. I was glad to see the cottage, but after tea and a meal felt fine again. Bob says snow blocked the road on Friday but a thaw has melted most of the fresh snow.

23 April. Student charities procession

At the end of Aberdeen University charities week, this was the big day for collecting money. Dressed as a clown, I walked to Footdee, Pittodrie and George Street. In the evening the collectors formed a procession. Crowds soon filled my tin. Whom did I spot in the crowd but the man who drove me to Monar in the snowstorm a fortnight ago? He is on holiday and down to Aberdeen for the day!

12 May.

Fine warm week. Pat and I are going to Iceland in July as transport to Spitsbergen is impossible. We begin preparations this week.

5 June. Watching eagles on Mar

Robert Carrick, senior lecturer in zoology at Aberdeen University, drove with me from his house at Torphins to a glen west of Braemar. There I showed him a nest of a golden eagle on a high crag and helped him start erecting a hide for photographing the eagles. The sole eaglet was gorged with food and unable to stand up. While we had lunch in the car, Robert was full of great schemes for what I am to do in my 4th year of the zoology course. He suggests a life history

AW's camp on Little Cairngorm, June 1949

of the golden eagle, and adding to my present stock of information by a detailed study of one pair for one season, as well as a close examination of their food, territories, etc. The idea thrills me to the bone – I never thought you could do a thing like that in 4th year, and he says if I got a really good series of photos in colour and black and white it would be tremendous. He talks even of my writing a Collins New Naturalist Monograph, and I am very keen on the idea if I could spend a season or two watching them every day. Tonight I was so excited about the prospect that it was a long time before I fell asleep.

11 June. At the eagle's nest

In the morning, both old birds had circled above Robert Carrick and me as we climbed to the eyrie, the hen quite close and showing her characteristic orange circular wing-marks. We had not seen them again and during a discussion after lunch, far down in the glen beside Robert's car, I ventured "probably she's on the skyline somewhere watching us". It was too incredible for words when seconds later as I glanced casually towards a distant skyline ridge I noticed a minute projection on it, and when putting binoculars on it found it to be an adult eagle, immobile and facing us at a distance of nearly 1½ miles. We decided to let her back at once and immediately drove down the glen and back to Torphins.

On a steep hill between Kincardine o' Neil and Torphins the car ran out of petrol and we had to shove it uphill for nearly ½ a mile – the last serious exertion of a pretty stiff day! Once over the top we free-wheeled for miles down to Torphins and after a meal I came into Aberdeen by bus.

Chapter 8. Iceland 1949

9 May. Decision to go to Iceland

Pat Sellar and I decided to go to north Iceland in July, because Norwegian coal company Store Norsk Spitsbergen Kulcompani do not give transport to Spitsbergen for an expedition.

24 June. To an Icelandic trawler at Aberdeen

Pat was to come at 1 pm to tell Wartle and me when the boat would leave, but did not turn up until 2, when we had filed in to a botany degree examination lasting till 5. The invigilator allowed him to tell us the boat would leave at 0200. After 5 I dashed to the bank to get travellers' cheques, next to the immigration office to stamp my passport, and then the Braemar bus-stop to collect skis and take them to the boat with Pat's help. Afterwards I caught a bus to my digs in Broomhill Road, had some supper, and then said goodbye to Broomhill Road and my respectable clothes as I left by bus, laden with a colossal pack. When dismounting in Union Street I had great difficulty controlling the unwieldy load and fell right over on to the pavement. As I rolled helplessly on my backside, two students came up to help me and walked with me to the boat at Point Law, one of them carrying my alpine rucksack. There I met Pat and Wartle. We waited up on deck until 2 am when the boat left, beside beautiful reflections of shore lights on the water. It is difficult to realise exams are all past. I had a feeling of great elation as the big trawler *Kaldbakur* finally left Aberdeen's lights behind and headed into the grey sea and the unknown that is ahead, packed with excitement.

27 June. Approaching Iceland

I awoke at 4 am feeling a lot better and had a look on deck, though there was nothing to see but fog and grey sea. Rain lashed down, so I hope this is not a foretaste of Iceland weather. Still, at 0900 a hazy peak appeared on our left through a smirr of rain – Iceland! Our excitement was terrific as we raced up to the bridge and put our binoculars on it. A grand peak it was, snow-splashed and rising out of fog, and as we headed north-west we saw a tremendous group of mountains to the south-west, rising above the flat lands of Melrakkasletta. Snowy from top to foot, they rose out of clouds and burned a beautiful soft gold in the sunlight. The most delicate shadow tints of soft blue filled their corries, and waves of silky gold snow on their crests soared high into blue sky. They were the most ethereal and beautiful things I have ever seen. Nothing could match their perfection across blue waters that sparkled in the sun. For nearly all the clouds had now gone and the sea was wonderfully calm. We passed north of the Arctic Circle at about 11 am and had for a long time the flat lands of Melrakkasletta on our left – what utter bleakness and desolation! There are homesteads in the most extraordinary positions, rickety corrugated iron and wooden buildings near desolate beaches, with the snowdrifts from last winter right to the water's edge. The boat passed many thousands of sea birds sitting on the calm water.

Then as we sailed nearer to the mountains we realised just what tremendous peaks they were. From them huge black cliffs dropped into the sea, threaded by high foaming waterfalls. The peaks lay under an enormous depth of snow. A glistening white sheet of it covered everything except the steepest ridges and buttresses. Vast cornices overhung the cliff edges, and every peak was a beautiful dome of folds of snow, deep and infinitely attractive. We passed a lovely glen there, a grassy place amongst a desert of scree, with a stream running down, fields of snow down to sea level, and the peaks above looking wilder and fiercer than any mountains I have ever seen. Now too we saw Grimsey, a barren low island away to the north, still streaked all over with last winter's snow. Evidently last winter was the hardest on record, and it was only a few weeks ago that the thaw came. Folk in these places must have had a very hard time.

Soon after this, by now afternoon, we saw that we were heading straight into the huge mass of mountains ahead, and what a thrill it was to move nearer and nearer to these vast steep-sided peaks.

Eventually there came an opening into Eyjafjörður, with high peaks dropping into the sea on either side, and away to the south appeared our glaciated mountains, immensely remote and hazy blue. The peak Kaldbakur and others east of the fjord entrance carried so much snow that the mountains seemed to be made of solid folds of snow, with great drifts right down to the beaches and a lonely farm almost surrounded by a level field of snow. In the distance we could see Akureyri town. The sun burned warmly from a deep blue sky flecked with white cloud, and glistened on massive 5000-foot peaks plastered with snow, rising out of snow-covered glaciers, and so near the town. Our excitement and anticipation were unbounded.

3 July. Vindheimajökull

After 9 I wakened Pat and Wartle, and at 10.45 we left for Vindheimajökull on a cold dull morning. On the lower slopes we saw a ptarmigan, a few cock snow buntings and a pair of golden plover, and ate crowberries preserved by snow since last year. Purple saxifrage had flowered. We walked on turf rich in pink moss campion, then by waterfalls and gorges to a corrie, and for 1000 feet up a steep narrow ridge on loose boulders and earth to a cliff-top gendarme.

Arriving on the plateau beside a great snowfield, we sank to the ankles in mud, but on reaching the snow put on skis. When the sun appeared, the light off the snow was blinding and the heat scorching. Striking views opened to the west, where dark clouds hung over wild hills. Our own peaks sparkled with deep unbroken snow where cloud shadows raced below a deep blue sky.

While leading, I landed in trouble where a stream bubbled from the snow. Suddenly I came into feet of slush and had to go back fast to avoid plunging in to the knees. We skied round it and then beside a slope showing avalanche signs, to a 1302-metre top. Pat and Wartle left their skis at 1200 metres but I carried mine to the top. Beyond, a ridge dropped 300 feet down loose boulders to curve in a pinnacled arete up to the 1451-metre conical summit above surrounding glaciers.

Snow fell and drifted, but stopped falling as we reached the summit. Far to the south-east rose the glaciers and peaks of Vatnajökull icecap, then Hofsjökull icecap cold blue, and nearer peaks sparkling in the sun. Clouds enveloped their summits and poured veils of snow across snowy buttresses, and the sun shot white shafts through coal-black cloud, a scene of immense grandeur.

At 5 we began to descend and then climb to the 1302-metre top. From it I had a very steep ski-run on snow sticky from today's fresh fall. Then we all skied across the plateau as dark clouds rolled in. Once the sun shone like a searchlight on a small circle of snow for a few yards around me. From the plateau a slippery descent followed in heavy sleet and we skied a mile on sticky snow to the moor.

Arriving hungry in camp at 9.15, we celebrated our highest yet peak with Mummery's blood, hot Bovril with a dash of glucose and some brandy, a prelude to a memorable meal. A wet cold evening set in by 11, but we have had a grand day.

7 July. Kaldbakur (cold back)

I woke at 8.45 to warm sunshine flooding the tent, and roused Pat and Wartle, which I have done every morning. After breakfast of porridge and milk, at 10.15 we carried skis in lovely glades of scrub birch up to 250 metres where redwings sang, and on grass with moss campion. At 350 metres we heard swishing as an Iceland gyrfalcon dropped close with black talons outstretched. A confiding purple sandpiper sat on four eggs.

Soon we skied up unbroken snow to the dome Þroskuldur, where Wartle and Pat decided to leave their skis. Beyond Þroskuldur I skied for nearly 200 metres altitude down a steep corrie, at one point in a funnel with a narrow gully which had to be taken straight and fast. At its foot I fell headlong on a soft patch but it was a grand run, followed by a glorious swoop into the foot of the corrie. Beyond, I climbed on ski, skirting an avalanche track. Then I climbed up boulders, seeing a mudslide taking off about 50 yards away. Ground below melting snow becomes saturated, and here it slid suddenly, carrying boulders, mud, and brown water in a spouting rush. Snow covered the east corrie down to a lake, deep under cracked muddy ice and snow.

At last I strode Kaldbakur above a big west corrie with loose cliffs overhung by cornices. I reached the 1167-metre top at 4.15 to see one of the best views I have ever had, out to the hazy blue Arctic Ocean, and wave after wave of mountains. To the east, snow covered 90% of ground on the Flateyjardalsheiði hills. I recognised our old friend Vindheimajökull. Peaks above Dalvik rose steeply across the shimmering blue fjord, and puffs of creamy cloud hung over them, casting blue shadows on spotless white slopes. It was warm even at 3900 feet, a perfect day.

Pat and Wartle appeared climbing the ridge to the peak Svinarhnukur ten metres lower and to the north. It had an edge of red rock with a cornice above a deep corrie, and an arete connected to Kaldbakur. After 45 minutes I

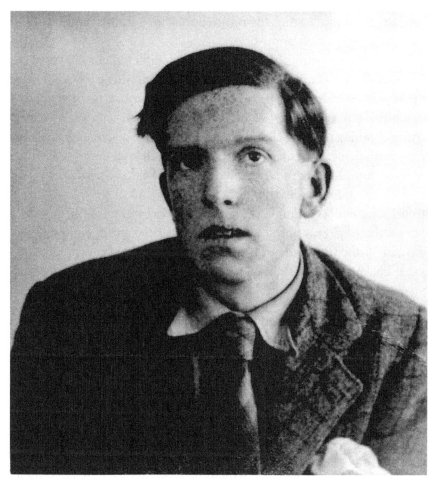

AW's passport photo for Iceland, May 1949

left, and, putting on skis at 3850 feet, swung downhill, slow enough to revel in the snowy peaks around. Soon though, the slope steepened and the surface became perfect spring snow. For 800 feet on a vast broad snowfield I descended in a series of stem turns, and here and there stem christianias on harder snow. Finally for another 200 feet I pointed the skis straight downhill and had a fast run at first, later turning stickier. From here my speed never exceeded 15 mph but I skied to 800 feet above the sea, down a steep snow-bridged gorge with great foaming waterfalls, in all a continuous run of over 3000 feet.

Coming into scrub birch, I strode in roasting sunshine and saw a golden plover with four lovely chicks and snow buntings singing. The fjord rippled in silvery light, golden plovers swung overhead singing, a redwing hopped into a birch tree with food, and Grenivik looked bonny with its white houses along the blue fjord. Arctic terns hawked insects close above the road.

At 7 I reached camp, and after baking pancakes had a brew of Bovril. I lazed till the others arrived at 9.15. Skiing on the lower slopes, they fell and their skis ran off a few times, once for nearly a mile. They thought it funny but I strongly advised using laces or straps tying the skis to their boots. After a big helping of cod and potato we had coffee and plum pudding. Now at midnight the sun shines a wine colour on Vindheimajökull's snow and the Dalvik hills are cold blue against a sky of duck-egg green. A last brew of cocoa is being prepared, then to the sleeping bags.

10 July. Kerling (old woman)

I roused Wartle and Pat at 8 to a morning of high wind, showers and sunny blinks, with fresh snow on Kerling. After breakfast of boiled cod and porridge, we left at 9.45, excellent going over moorland and rocky ground. Many whimbrels, golden plover and meadow pipits called, a few dunlins trilled and snipe drummed, and in rocky places a few snow buntings sang. We saw fledged snow buntings and pipits, and an Arctic skua. Blooms of mountain avens with white petals and orange centres dotted the moor like snowflakes, and sea thrift grew commonly. For a few minutes we rested on turf, basking in the sun and listening to whimbrels singing.

Now we walked up grass and a rocky ridge to Bondi, a sharp rock nipple. Steep walking led to 4500 feet where a gale roared through a funnel, but as we moved over easy pinnacles it began to ease. The route led through a lane between rock walls rising to sharp needles. Afterwards we descended rock rubble and fresh snow to a col, where Kerling soared above, with a big cliff rising to a summit plateau wreathed in mist. It rose from a snow-covered glacier with dirty crevassed ice, leading to Glerardalur.

By a steep slope of loose scree we climbed round a rock corner on hard neve and up to a narrow neck under a massive block of rotten rock. Wartle narrowly missed hitting Pat's head when he dislodged a rock, so I advised careful light footwork. Because Pat and Wartle deemed it unsafe to cross a scree ledge above a big drop to the glacier, we climbed the block into the mist, over rocks beautifully iced up. In front, I swung down rotten rock on a little steep cliff for 30 feet, then along a neck, and up towards a summit looking magnified by mist.

After waiting five minutes I returned to find Pat and Wartle sitting. They thought it too difficult, but I encouraged Pat to descend the little cliff, for it did not exceed moderate standard. I descended the cliff again, and he followed more slowly. Then up the last gully I climbed swiftly to the plateau and across a broad cornice to the cairn at the cliff edge, my highest peak (1538 metres). In dense mist, snow whirled past on a bitter wind and rime plastered the cairn. As I left, I met Pat 50 yards away, heading for the summit. After climbing the little cliff, I stood beside Wartle at 4 o'clock. I wished I had taken the rope, which would have given him confidence. I am sorry, as it was his wish that we come to Kerling. After waiting ten minutes for Pat, we descended a few hundred feet of loose scree to a snowfield in Kvarnardalur. We ran fast down the snow and on a steeper slope had a lovely glissade for 2000 feet.

The moor gave an easy fast descent. Beautiful cushions of moss campion carpeted a flat area in all colours from white to blood-red, a wonderful sight. The only flower on the ridge was purple saxifrage. It has been a very enjoyable and interesting day, and not tiring. We arrived at camp at 6.30 and soon had hot Bovril, followed by boiled cod, potato soup made with fish water, then coffee with pancakes that I baked, eaten straight off the pan. This was our last night together.

11 July. To Bægisardalur

I called reveille at 8 and saw fresh snow on Kerling down to 4500 feet. We are sorry to leave this fine spot, with a waterfall nearby and violets at the tent door. After walking a mile we got a lift in a lorry to Akureyri, where we bought food. A policeman said "You have not shaved for a very long time", and then offered the police station's grassy yard as a camp site. He pointed out a Scot from Bridge of Weir, who is renovating the golf course. The Scot told the policeman "watch these Aberdonians, they throw away their money like a man without arms", whereupon the policeman as a joke threatened him with jail as punishment. An old man outside Kea (Cooperative Store) laughed on seeing me, no wonder, for I have a big hole in my trousers. A man at the shipping office did not know when the trawler *Svalbakur* will stop on the way to Grimsby, but said to call in 5 to 6 days. This will cut the time I have left for climbing.

At our base camp at Kifsa near Akureyri, we ate a snack and divided the remaining food. My pack weighed 65 lb. As we tramped down for the last time and listened to whimbrels bubbling, redshanks, ravens, dunlin, ptarmigan and other birds that made Kifsa so interesting, I could not help thinking of events since we arrived a fortnight ago, so much that it seems like months. Pat and Wartle were to walk to Akureyri and go by bus to Reykjavik tomorrow. I was to go to Ytri Bægisa to climb. A lorry came, going my way, and stopped. Pat, Wartle and I shook hands, wished good luck, and then I was off and away, sorry to go, for I shall miss their company. The driver took me to the end of the Hjalteyri road, where I had a lift for three kilometres and a walk of two, and then a lift to Ytri Bægisa in a lorry going to Reykjavik.

I walked past Sydri Bægisa, with its big buildings as Icelandic farms go. Then I climbed into the west side of Bægisardalur. A strap of my army pack came off because the rivets fell out. I camped on turf and crowberry plants by a foaming stream. Mountains tower above, with much snow on them and glaciers. What I shall do I do not know, probably nothing too ambitious now that I am alone and nobody knows I am here. It is 8 pm and I am off for a short walk. Strolling above the gorge that leads to Bægisarjökull glacier, I found five cock snow buntings singing and a hen feeding a fledged chick. Blinks of sunshine are beautiful but dark clouds hide the tops. I can only hope for good weather for the next three days.

12 July. A peak near Hafrarhnukur

Sunlight flooding the tent woke me at 6.45 to a magnificent morning. Not a cloud dimmed the sky and I saw all the peaks. Finest was Krummi to the west, a beautiful steep cone above sparkling snowfields. A shoulder of Vindheimajökull towered, split by great ravines, and Haafjall's fantastic knife-edge ridge rose to sharp high needles.

Leaving before 8, I walked through a rushy bog alive with screeching dunlin, redshank, golden plover, and whimbrel with young. Many ringed plover with chicks on shingle gave alarm calls, and I saw two Arctic terns, a great black-backed gull, and meadow pipits feeding fledged young. The spate shingles, the blue water on the river, and fantastic rock peaks made a grand setting.

Already at 9.30 the sun shone warmly, so after dumping my jersey I walked up turf rich with flowers. A pair of wheatears had four fledged young and a meadow pipit nest six eggs, and many golden plover called. A long pull up the ridge led to easy going over vast stony plateaux. The last 1500 feet gave heavy walking on spring snow, though it would have been beautiful for skiing. On the last part, yesterday's fresh snow had frozen and I cut steps. I was glad to sit in fairly warm sunshine on the 1337-metre summit, unnamed on my map but north-east of Hafrarhnukur.

The view surpassed any I have had in Iceland. The cairn stood on the edge of a snow-filled corrie overlooked by cornices and rock ridges. To the north rose a big peak, its gullies filled by snow and offering 3000-foot glissades. Below, a snowy corrie led to a green valley with no houses and steep snowy mountains on its far side. Puffs of orange and purple cloud hung round them, trailing blue shadows over the snow. Across the valley rose snowy twin-topped Hafrarhnukur, and beyond it many peaks shimmered in the heat, their snows a dazzling white.

Further south I saw black cliffs, spotless plateaux and corrie glaciers glinting green in the sun. Beyond the rock peak of Haafjall and tangled snowy ridges rose Langjökull icecap with cliffs of green ice. I looked past the blue fjord to snowy Kaldbakur, and many miles away the mountains near Myvatn and beyond, where cumulus clouds hung top heavy above their own blue shadows. It was a climber's dreamland, and a ski-mountaineer's, for the peak to the north-east had a snowfield for 3000 feet and 2000-foot runs abounded on every side.

I thought of Pat and Wartle in the hot Reykjavik bus and wondered if they knew what they were missing by going to a big town. The thought of traversing a rock peak and up a snow gully to the fine peak of Hafrarhnukur tempted me, with a steep 2000-foot glissade on descent, but I felt it would be unduly risky. I am taking enough risks by climbing alone here. Once on the way up, as I sweated on the snowfield, looking at the immensity of world and sky, and listening to dull throbbing silence, I had a slight chill of fear, which I have not had in Scotland for a long time. But it vanished quickly and I enjoyed myself greatly for the rest of the day. If only Tom Weir had been here, how much more we could have done, climbs up rocky ridges, huge glissades and fine skiing.

View west from Landafjall on AW's second climb alone in Iceland, 13 July 1949

After half an hour on top, I left at 1.30 for a very fast run down loose snow, hindered only by some stretches of soft mud. Then a glorious swoop of a standing glissade led for 500 feet into the Oddstadaa gorge, where I ate a snack by a waterfall. The ration for each of us on a climb has been a square of chocolate, a spoonful of glucose, a date, and a slice of bread and cheese (or a tin of sardines for three of us). However, plenty of food remained at the end of our trip and I did not spare it on this, my heaviest day in Iceland so far. I had three squares of chocolate, four dates, three slices of rye bread and cheese, and a tin of sardines.

Down I walked into a lovely green valley and arrived at camp rather tired at 5, but after a meal felt fit, save for some sunburn pain. Now at 7.45 I write this outside the tent in roasting sun. The sky is undimmed blue, save for a tuft of white cloud above Krummi. The snow looks silvery in the sun and deep blue in the shade, and soft sunlight floods the valley. Only yards away, a fledged snow bunting pipes incessantly to be fed and the cock has just fed it. I have snow buntings and the roar of the river for company. It seems ages since yesterday. At 10 pm I finished darning. Thread has run out but I patched holes in my socks with sticking plaster sewn to the socks.

On a lovely night, the sun has sunk behind a mountain but burns red on Vindheimajokull. A cloud sea tinged with pink and mauve fills the fjord and above it the snows of Kaldbakur are rosy against a pale gold sky.

13 July. Landafjall

I slept poorly due to sunburn pain, but woke at 7.30 with the pain gone. Dense mist filled the gorge, but the sun appeared through a hole so I knew it would be a good day. After breakfast, sun flooded the peaks across the valley. Blue wraiths hung idly in windless air above the corries, and the snowy peaks looked huge, rising out of clouds. The stream dashed blue and silver in the sun. I never hoped to get weather like this. At 8.50 I am about to leave in hot sunshine.

Later, at 5.30 I am back after a wonderful day and a cooked meal. I went up Bægisardalur on its west side, along the top of a gorge with black crags and clouds of spray. Then I strode on turf rich with flowers and birds, where I lay 20 minutes to watch whimbrel calling close above, golden plover piping, snipe drumming, and a cock snow bunting feeding two fledglings. I decided to climb Trollafjall, rising over 3000 feet in snow slopes and rock ridges from the gorge. First, though, I had to cross the river. Time after time I hopped on to boulders, but always a very long jump loomed ahead with a tremendous roar of water below. A slip would be perdition. After clambering among huge boulders upstream for nearly a mile I gave up.

Instead I chose Landafjall, a 1236-metre peak on the west side, so I climbed out of the gorge for 2500 feet to the skyline. A spectacular view appeared as I reached the ridge and looked into Oxnadalur 3300 feet below, the road a thin ribbon of white, a few dot-like crofts, and on the far side a range of peaks sparkling in the sun, a wilderness of snow and splintered rock. I continued along a narrow rock ridge towards the summit, where views were even better.

Quite close, the corrie of Hegarskal with beetling black cliffs led to snowfields overlooked by cornices. Not far off soared Bægisarjökull glacier, a broad shimmering sheet so deep that its black rocky peaks seemed almost buried. To the east, Trollafjall looked immense above a steep front into the valley, with rock ridges and splintered cliffs scored by huge gullies offering 3000-foot glissades, great tracts of scree and gravel, and vast snowfields.

From Landafjall I looked across to the weird rock peak Haafjall and below it a beautiful lake Hraunsvatn, deep blue in the sun and reflecting the snowfields. Views of peaks at the top of Barkardalur surpassed yesterday's, spotless plateaux with short snow-plastered cliffs leading to glaciers and snowfields, down to brown valleys with steep slopes of rock and scree scored by snow gullies, a scene of wilderness. North-east rose Kaldbakur, still with folds of snow almost to sea level, a grand picture with the deep blue of the fjord below.

Continuing along to Bægisarjökull, I walked easily on the glacier because all the ice lay invisible under a thick coat of firm snow, and then returned to the Landafjall plateau. I left the top and had a magnificent standing glissade for 1000 feet, starting ten yards from the summit, and when the slope eased near the foot I lay on my back and shot down faster. Then there followed a walk of 100 yards over a stony plateau, where a purple sandpiper called in alarm. This led to another glissade for 500 feet, steep and fast even standing, so I had to brake with the axe. Another short walk brought me to the last glissade for 300 feet down an easier slope, so I sat down and shot happily downhill. Although melting snow soaked me, I soon dried in hot sunshine.

By sheep paths I walked to the tent through a rocky tract moving with singing snow buntings, and a few golden plover, snipe and pipits. Whimbrel bubbled above the flower-dotted moor, and amongst dwarf willow, blaeberry and birch scrub flitted huge numbers of moths. I reached the tent at 4.15 after a very fine day, scarcely much tired.

After a big meal, at 6.45 I lie on crowberry plants by the tent, still basking in roasting sunshine. After patching all holes in my socks with sewn-on sticking plaster I bathed my feet in the stream. At 9.15 it is a perfect night, not a cloud in sight. Krummi's snows are suffused with warm creamy tones and Haafjall's rock needles stand blue-black against a sky of palest blue. It will be early to bed tonight. This is the very essence of adventure.

14 July. Trollafjall

After a good sleep I woke at 7 to find dense fog. I slept till 8.45 when I rose to find frost on the grass and then cooked breakfast. At 9.30 the sun broke through on Haafjall and scarves of cloud hung around its blue buttresses like smoke from a fire.

At 5.30 I am home to camp again after a very fine day. I crossed the river Bægisa at the bridge and climbed the 1471-metre Trollafjall. At first I walked up meadows full of whimbrel, golden plover, meadow pipits and snipe, with a song chorus up to 2300 feet. A few wheatears chattered from boulders. Where the slope steepened I found many snow buntings, the only birds at 3000 feet apart from a few golden plover. I saw many fledged buntings being fed, cocks singing close on every prominent boulder, and a total of over 50 cocks on this short stretch.

Then there came an easy climb for nearly 4000 feet to the top of the north flank. The views surpassed any so far. Masses of white fog filled Bægisardalur and cloud wisps streamed up around me, causing rainbows and sun halos. Bægisarjökull loomed immensely high out of fog. Further north-east, dove-grey cloud filled valleys and fjord, and snowy Kaldbakur stuck its white top out like a boat on the sea. Near me the hot sun soon evaporated the mist. Cold wafts of cloud rolled up the vast corrie, to vanish as they breasted the ridge.

An interesting arete swept up beside a snow cornice, but I found the rock loose and once got a fright when I put my feet on a hold in a rock wall and a large piece crumbled. At 1 o'clock I trod the summit of Trollafjall and gazed on as fine a panorama as any mountaineer could wish. Across a snow-covered glacier rose Vindheimajokull's twin peaks. Further round shimmered Kerling, the snows of its cliffs and glacier a soft blue, rimmed by a gold cornice. Around Hafrarhnukur and snowy peaks near it, a few blue clouds twisted in windless air. To the east lay the deep blue fjord and north of it creamy-blue cloud over the Arctic Ocean. As I stood looking beyond the valley, now tiny and far below, past the vast waves of snow peaks to the cloud over the ocean, I had an even more passionate desire to go further north and see even more exciting country. Although Iceland has given me of her best for the whole trip and especially these last three days, it whets my appetite for wilder places and more adventure, in the real Arctic.

Lying in sunshine, I looked at the view for an hour. As I left, I noticed beyond Haafjall a snowy plateau glowing creamy in the sun, so bright above hazy lower slopes that it seemed like no earthly mountain, but an ethereal one hanging in blue sky. Above it, orange-coloured spears of cloud threw soft blue shadows on the snow.

To descend I could take steep snow for 2600 feet or a steep ridge of loose scree. I decided to glissade, after a little hesitation considering the risk for a lone man if things went wrong. But I felt only a trifle nervous as I clambered over the cornice ten yards from the top and gingerly moved down on the first part of this colossal slope.

Things went well and for the first 500 feet I had a glorious swoop of a standing glissade, though I had to brake all the time. After this the slope eased and the snow became softer, so I sat down and moved happily down at about 15 mph. On an icy bit in the middle, suddenly I shot fast downhill over hard snow, but gained control by rolling over with toes and elbows dug in and the axe braking. Gradually I slowed, and after 300 feet of hard snow the slope steepened into granular snow, leading towards a broad gully. Remaining seated I shot down here, feeling on top of the world, and when at the edge of the gully I saw it led for another clear 1500 feet at a less steep angle I whooped with joy. More confidently I let myself go at full length, a glorious fast slide for 1000 feet. The last 500 feet led down a steep gorge full of hard snow, just right for a fast standing glissade. At the bottom of it I looked back at the peak far above, and the long track of the finest and most thrilling glissade I have ever had.

It had been glorious fun. Although melting snow had soaked me completely, I spread my clothes to dry for half an hour in the hot sun. Snow buntings sang and fed fledged young, and as I walked back I saw buntings nearly all the time.

A sheep track led across steep gravel and scree slopes above the gorge, but it was very loose and a couple of nasty slips made me slow down and take great care. All the way home on the green moor I had bubbling whimbrel, golden plover, an odd snipe, meadow pipits, wheatears and singing snow bunting for company. Bird life on these moors is far richer than in Scotland. The moors teem with birds. The sheep track crossed a green meadow dotted white with flowers, and moss campion flared red masses of bloom.

As I walked towards my tent I thought this was the end of all the adventure packed into the last few days. The rest of my time may be interesting but that extra spice of adventure will be missing. I have had my full share, though. Every night since I left Pat and Wartle what seems ages ago, I have felt that nervous elation that comes with anticipation of grand adventure, a feeling I previously had strongly only once, before my New-Year crossing of Lairig Ghru on skis alone. I never dreamed I could have had three such magnificent days in succession. They have been wonderful for me among the loneliest, highest, most desolate and yet most thrilling mountains I have ever set foot on. The last three days have been among the finest of my life.

Hungrily I arrived at camp to eat most of my remaining food. Now at 6.45 I lie among flowers in hot sunshine, looking at mountains sparkling with gold and blue light. A cock snow bunting has just crossed the gorge, a flash of silver between the sun and me. I thought I would feel the lack of Pat and Wartle's company but curiously I do not, and am at peace with the world.

9.25 pm. The glissades have worn holes in my trousers, so I spent an hour mending them. After cocoa and biscuits I am ready for bed on a glorious evening. The tops scintillate against a frosty sky, cloudless save for a wisp of mist hanging over Hafrarhnukur, a wisp transformed by the sun into a flare of silver like a diamond.

15 July. To Akureyri

At 9 I packed up, sorry to leave such a grand place, but high cloud had come in, so I have been lucky over the last three days. My pack weighed over 50 lb, awkward to carry with a strap loose, so I sat at the roadside, confident of a lift. I waited three and a half hours without seeing a vehicle, so started walking. After three miles I descended into a marshy valley full of birds, with a pair of greylag geese, nesting great black-backed gulls, three ravens chased by whimbrels, dunlin screeching everywhere, a few Arctic terns, and many meadow pipits, redshank, golden plover and snipe. By now, heavy clouds wreathed the hills, and rain and sleet fell. Four miles from Ytri Bægisa the first car appeared, and, wonders, stopped. A Reykjavik couple asked me in and I sat with the rucksack on my knee. I seemed to float in comfort on a soft seat to Akureyri, showered by kind words and pieces of Icelandic chocolate.

In Akureyri I visited the shipping office, to be told that the trawler *Svalbakur* is not due till at least the 20th, so I shall have to spend longer in town than I wished. The policeman on duty at the police station showed me round the station and kindly told me to use it as I pleased, and helped erect my tent on a patch of grass at the back door. Police constable 7, Jon Sigurgeirsson, now appeared. Chortling with laughter, he poked his head in at my tent door and asked me to come into his office for coffee. A good English speaker and happy man, he told me to use the station as my home.

Later, senior officer Jon Benediktsson invited me to his cottage. While we had coffee, he played records. He showed me his piano, mandolin, violin and accordion, all of which he plays, and his extensive library with many German, English, Swedish, and Danish books as well as Icelandic. He speaks English, Swedish, German, Danish and Norwegian well, and keeps in close touch with international events and politics.

After driving me to the police station, he left me with Jon Sigurgeirsson, who gave me cakes and coffee. When I mentioned seeing Vatnajökull, he said he had driven by jeep across the desert to its north edge and climbed Iceland's second highest mountain there. Next time I visit Akureyri, he said he would like to go there with me. By now it was midnight, with beautiful light down the fjord, and we went in his jeep to the shore. The sun lay behind clouds with jet black centres, turning to gold and then blood-red near the frilled edges. On the calm mirror of the fjord, the water glowed bright orange-red. Along the hillsides, dove-grey streams of cloud hung, merging into the mysterious grey of the peaks, except where a shaft of sun turned them to fire. Hundreds of fishing Arctic terns screamed as they traced fluttering shadows over the vast pool of red water in front of us, an experience never to be forgotten.

Afterwards Jon drove the jeep to an old power station at Glerard gorge, where the river boils furiously round black recesses in the rock. Clouds of spray hit us, coming from the turbulent cauldron. On the way back to the station he

Landafjall from north flank of Trollafjall, 14 July 1949

suddenly said "Can I make you frightened"? He turned his jeep up a steep slope towards the main road, and we looked at the sky all the way up.

At the station he offered me a jail cell for the night. However, another constable said he had seen so many drunks in town on this Saturday night that he might need to lock a few up. Still, I will be in the cells tomorrow night. It is now 0100 on Sunday after a fine evening.

20 July. Vindheimajökull

Constable Jon Sigurgeirsson shook me out of deep sleep in my tent outside the jail at 0300, saying it was a fine morning. As soon as I rose, he told me to finish the coffee in his flask and eat the cake left in his bag. Next he offered to drive over a third of the way to Vindheimajokull. We went in a lorry on a fresh bright morning, with sunlight flooding the fjord. The sun turned the cliffs an extraordinary purple and the snow a soft gold against a pale green sky. Mellow light played on the moorland grasses.

After he left I walked up a track to a ski hut, enjoying the morning softness. Water droplets glistened on grass. Golden plover piped and two flapped in song, and I saw a few dunlin, whimbrel, ptarmigan and snow buntings, but most whimbrel and redshank had left. The beautiful tints vanished as golden night became day.

A tiring climb followed up the ridge north of Hliderskal corrie, quite a sweat with the skis. No wind stirred the calm air and a cloud layer formed quickly. Moss campion bloomed, turning one part of the slope rosy with glowing red pads. Grand views opened. The fjord reflected the snowy peaks, and far beyond there rose the Myvatn hills, dark blue, and backed by black and gold clouds now pierced by sun shafts, mysterious and attractive. Vatnajökull icecap stood full in the sun above dark clouds, and the sun turned the spotless snows of surrounding peaks to blue, white, and gold. Vatnajökull must be a wonderful place and it may not be long before I go there with Jon.

I reached the plateau at 7.15 after three and a half hours from the bridge below Logmannshlið. A climb to the 1302-metre peak revealed great snow melt since we skied here on 3 July. Big areas are snow-free, and snowy basins carry great pools of water. On my skis I shot on good spring snow into the main basin, which held a small snow-covered lake beside a moraine. I skied up to the flat top that leads to Vindheimajökull by an arete. The air was clammy and completely windless, and the silence more intense than I have experienced for a long time. Vainly the sun tried to pierce motionless black clouds.

Suddenly I heard ticking behind me, as loud as a clock and regular. For a minute it beat exact time with the seconds of my watch, coming from above the snow on the edge of the rocky plateau. Removing my skis, I found that the noise beat regularly from underground. Feeling slightly bewildered I put the skis on to face a 750-foot slope. I swooped down steep and fast, and after zigzags pointed the skis straight to the lake. There followed a grand run, very fast on good snow, but yet not as good as we have had on Ben Macdui in spring. A perfect deep layer of spring snow seems less frequent here, because of little freezing during the mostly sunny night.

I crossed the blue ice of the glacier and after skiing slightly downhill, removed the skis again. I slapped them to knock off loose snow and the noise echoed from the far side of the basin. After the echoes came a buzzing in the air from the direction of the far side, as though from a bee close by. Patches of sun lit the snow like torches, unmoving. Across yellow boulders that crumbled to dust at a kick of the boot, I hastened towards the plateau edge. My hair began to creep. Though unafraid, nevertheless I felt puzzled and uneasy. Suddenly, ticking began at longer intervals out of the air a few yards away. My hair crept and rose against my hand. After staying a minute I lifted my skis to walk away, but my hair rose again and I felt a chill in the air. I reasoned that static electricity was causing the noises and making my hair stand on end, and, given the sultry conditions and black clouds, there was a risk of lightning.

As I left the plateau to face a snowy gully, the strange feelings and noises vanished completely. I forgot them in the joys of a magnificent standing glissade, down for 1200 feet, a very fine swoop. The sun came out for an hour and I strode down the moor. A snow bunting fed a fledgling, another sang, and a golden plover with young piped in alarm. A long tramp down to Akureyri followed. I was hungry, for I had only some dry rye bread for the climb. While walking I fell asleep for an instant, enough to make me stagger, close to falling in a heap on the dusty road.

At camp I had porridge and coffee, and slept two hours. Jon said the trawler *Svalbakur* will leave tomorrow afternoon for Grimsby. In an invigorating north wind I walked to the shore, how different from the clammy air earlier.

As usual I waited for Jon Sigurgeirsson, who drove me to his lodgings, where at midnight he gave me coffee and cake. I told him of the odd events on Vindhemajökull, and we thought static electricity had caused them. He said most small birds at Myvatn such as wagtails and pipits had died in a severe storm in early June. A blizzard and hard frost came even at sea level, and whimbrel, golden plover and other waders crowded the estuary below his lodgings, where many died. He said snowy owls nest in the deserts and great numbers of greylag geese at lakes in the inner highlands.

When the talk came to Myvatn, he said "The people there eat duck eggs at all stages, even when there is a little bird in them. Better still, they store the eggs and eat them later, maybe months or a year later. Of course they smell very bad, but they are very good, just like cheese" After a fine talk we returned to the police station. Then I said goodbye to my kind friend and retired to the jail cell at 0130 for a good sleep.

21 July. Leaving Iceland

I rose late to find a beautiful day of sun and blue sky. After breakfast of porridge, cod and coffee in my tent on grass outside the police station, I was startled when a policeman came at 11.00 to announce that the trawler *Svalbakur* had docked and would leave at 13.30. A frantic rush began, to the quay and trawler to arrange a lift, the Customs office to stamp my passport, and back to the police station to pack up. On seeing my heavy load, Jon Benediktsson offered to drive me to the boat in his old car, and presented me with a souvenir booklet on Iceland, kindness to the very last. At 13.45 I said goodbye to him and Akureyri as the *Svalbakur* (chilly back) moved on to the fjord in grand weather. A beautiful new trawler built at Hall & Son in Aberdeen, this is only her second trip. The boat has many small luxuries such as an electric light for each bunk. I had not had lunch, so I enjoyed the tasty cakes and coffee. We had a pleasant

On way up to north flank, looking south, 14 July 1949

journey down the fjord, with the Dalvik peaks looking spectacular, rising out of banks of sea fog and still heavily splashed with snow, to sea level in places. I was in tears as I looked at them. At supper I dug into an excellent meal of mutton, potatoes, carrots, sardines, bread and cheese, followed by more cakes and coffee. Out on the open sea it was still calm as the snowy Flateyjardalsheidi hills dropped into a haze of gold.

22 July. At sea on the trawler Svalbakur

At 1 am I woke feeling rotten and soon after was very sick. My meals of yesterday landed in the Arctic Ocean, joined by those of Icelandic passengers. The boat heaved in a heavy swell, and fog added to the dismal outlook. I slept most of today, taking an occasional nip of brandy.

23 July. First sight of Scotland

At 2 am we passed a lighthouse flashing on Faeroe. It was sunny today, with less of a swell. We sighted Orkney at 7, and thereafter the swell began to die. At 9.30 I went on deck to see Hoy, where light cloud hung on the Kame. Homeland again! An hour later it was quite dark, very different from Iceland, and lighthouses flashed on every side.

24 July. Off Aberdeenshire

I woke at 6.30 to find a grand morning of sun and blue sky, and the sea like glass, quite smooth. We were off Rattray Head, and I could pick out Mormond Hill, St Combs and other places, and further south the hazy but unmistakable outline of Bennachie. Herring gulls yelled loudly. It was good to see north-east Scotland again. Later we went out of sight of land, and at noon the sea was still calm and we were off Berwickshire.

28 July. To Grimsby

At 5 I woke to find the day breaking on the Humber estuary, and the boat not moving. An English pilot told me that the skipper was waiting to get a better price for his fish tomorrow. It seems late, however, as the temperature in the fish hold has risen to 43 F and the fish must be deteriorating. The younger Icelandic passengers excitedly pointed to woods and said "skog", Icelandic for a wood, for they had never seen such big woods. After many delays we tied up in dock at 5 pm, but by the time the immigration and customs officers had looked over the boat it was 7. A day of cloudless skies and roasting heat had given way to gloom, and as a London student and I walked down Grimsby's dismal streets a thunderstorm broke with torrential rain. The last train to London had gone and it was now too late for me to get money from the post office, so we returned to the *Svalbakur* for the night.

29 July. To Glasgow

I woke at 6 to a loud racket above, from machines unloading the fish. The stench of three-week old cod pervaded the deck, and the London student and I then slithered among ice and cod in the fish market, glad to get away, for the harbour here is an unpleasant place. I saw him off on the train to London. Knowing I had hardly any money left, he generously paid for my tea in Grimsby yesterday and gave me two shillings this morning to tide me over. While I waited for the post office to open, a young policeman asked for my "credentials". After I had shown him my passport and explained my plans, he said "sorry for asking, but you cut a pretty suspicious figure in that rig-out", as he pointed to my rucksack, ice-axe and old clothes. He showed me where to get a cheap breakfast, with tea, fried eggs and bread for a shilling. Many Grimsby down-and-outs who slept on the street were there, anxious to know "Wayre was you in the stoam last noit?" (Where were you in the storm last night).

At last the post office opened, and I got Dad's registered letter with £4. I bought a ticket to Glasgow and sent my skis home by rail to get them out of the way. Now I await the train, another scorching day. I thought of the good climb I would be missing today on the Glencoe hills, because of the delays yesterday. At 10.30 I caught a slow train to Doncaster, passing uninteresting flat farmland. It was nice to see swallows again. A quick dash at Doncaster got me a seat in a crowded carriage to York, but the 60-lb rucksack is an awkward burden, and once while I shouldered it my camera became stuck, a rucksack strap broke, and a hole was torn in my anorak. After a quick snack at York I caught a fast train non-stop to Glasgow, packed to the limit. It pulled into Glasgow at 9 pm after a roasting day of cloudless skies.

At the snack bar I paid for tea and six big sandwiches, and then phoned Dad at Onich, arranging to meet tomorrow at Bridge of Orchy for a climb. After buying a ticket to Bridge of Orchy I had less than three shillings left, so decided

On north flank of Trollafjall, 14 July 1949

to spend the night in the waiting room. Eventually it closed, and when I walked to Central Station I found its waiting room closed too. A friendly policeman based in the station showed me a compartment in a train due to leave at 0700, so I bedded down in comfort.

30 July. To Bridge of Orchy

At 5 am I woke and had a long chat with the policeman and his two colleagues. Then I walked to Queen Street Station, where a weighing machine showed I had lost more than a stone on the Iceland trip. I boarded the empty Fort William train at 5.30, now a drizzly morning with low cloud. I had only two shillings and seven pence left, so could afford only porridge and a cup of tea at the station restaurant. At Bridge of Orchy I came off the train in lashing rain, and retreated to a sheltered corner of the platform, where I lit my stove and started to brew a pot of porridge. At that moment Dad appeared and drove me down to the local hotel for breakfast. Auntie Else was there and her dog Princie went crazy with rage when it saw me, snarling and snapping. Elsie was in fits of laughter at my appearance, and said I must get a photograph taken.

After seeing her off on a train to Glasgow, we drove to Fort William. Rain and lowering mist shrouded Rannoch Moor, but we had a good sight on a wee lochan there, three black-throated divers. In Fort William a photographer took a photo of me. Then I lost my first beard as a hairdresser removed it with electric clippers and gave me my first haircut in ten weeks, followed by a shampoo. I felt quite chilled on the head afterwards. In the evening we went to a Gaelic concert and enjoyed it thoroughly. The audience shouted for more and more Gaelic songs till nearly midnight. Afterwards, the comfort of a soft bed was a strange new luxury. Iceland seemed far away, but July 1949 there has been the best month of my life so far.

Chapter 9. Late 1949

10 August. Cairnsmore in Galloway

At Ayr I am staying with Auntie Else. Taking a bus to a point near Carsphairn, we climbed Cairnsmore. A day of blue sky and billowing white clouds was right for visiting these rolling hills, with cloud shadows chasing over big moors. In the afternoon the sun began to hide behind dark clouds as veils of rain swept over. We discussed politics, religion, psychology and journalism. Returning in great form to Carsphairn, we had tea and caught a bus to Ayr in pelting rain.

16 August. Goatfell

It was a fine morning, so Else woke me early. Laden with camping gear and food, we went by bus and foot to Ayr harbour to board *The Marchioness of Graham* at 9 o'clock. We had enough food for feasts, but several discarded small herring on the quay side were a good find. During a bonny run across to Brodick we saw many gannets and Manx shearwaters.

Through rich woodland we walked the road to Brodick Castle in unusual heat, but once we had picked a good camp site on a slope of a clearing and eaten a fine meal we felt ready for Goatfell. Else had not considered going to the top, but we walked up a rough boggy path, taking frequent rests, past shoals of tourists wearing tennis shoes. It was just the day for it, warm sun, blue sky with fleecy white clouds, and a riot of purple heather everywhere.

At 2500 feet the path ended among big boulders and the slope steepened. Here Else stopped and would go no further, dismayed by the declivity on the far side, a pair of croaking ravens flapping wildly over the summit, the silver clouds scudding close overhead, and the summit "like a black dungeon" she said. I raced to the top and had a memorable view. On the far side, sharp ridges and rock peaks of granite glistened wet from recent rain. I will come back some day to climb these ridges. The hills of Donegal stood clear and the islands of west Scotland rose jet black from a pool of gold that was the Atlantic. Beyond a blue sea to the east, Ayrshire seemed almost at our feet, a land of woods, fields and rolling green hills, while northwards rose the Cumbrae islands and the lower Highlands clear as crystal.

Boulder-hopping, I ran down to Else and we commenced a slow steady descent to camp as the sun sank behind the hills. It was good to see my tent again, and soon we lit a fire, and then grilled kippers, herrings, sausages and tomatoes on the red embers. I followed this by heating a can of soup on the fire, and then we ate bread and honey. At dusk we sat outside drinking tea.

17 August. At Brodick Castle

A dull day dawned, and hordes of flies and midges set upon us as soon as we looked outside. The answer was to smoke them out by getting a fire going. We grilled kippers on the embers as No 1 feature of the menu again, and sat in the smoke while we stuck into a grand breakfast. Then, as Elsie felt stiff after Goatfell, we roamed the woods all forenoon instead of climbing up the hills. The thickets of rhododendron must make this place a show when the flowers are out. Through dank plantations choked with bracken we returned to camp. In the afternoon we walked to a cafe for tea, and then back to camp for another fire and a feast of ember-cooked soup, tomato, kipper, herring, sausage, and bacon, followed by bread with honey, biscuits and tea. Rain drove us in early, but we lay talking till midnight.

18 August. On Arran

We awoke late to see heavy drizzle, so I cooked breakfast on my stove inside the tent. As soon as we went out, hordes of midges annoyed us until we had packed up. After walking to Brodick, we took a bus over hills covered with heather and bracken to Whiting Bay, where we sat by the shore until the boat came, discussing many topics. We reached Ayr after 6 and tramped to Elsie's house at Auchendoon Crescent after a very fine trip.

23 September. To Beauly

Yesterday I planned to go to Glen Strathfarrar, and this morning Stewart decided to come at the last minute, so we had a rush. Dad on a business trip took us to Inverurie, and we walked miles out the Huntly road thumbing vainly for lifts, later boarding a bus reaching Inverness at 7 pm. After cold pies and lukewarm tea in the station we caught a bus to Beauly. We walked for some time searching unsuccessfully for a doss around The Toll until a German ex-POW farm worker showed us to a barn and asked us to have tea with him and his Scots wife. We bedded at 10 in straw, which soon rustled with rats and mice near our rucksacks. It was pitch dark and we had no torch.

24 September. To Glen Strathfarrar

After a poor sleep due to the rats and mice, we were relieved to find our rucksacks intact. In a shed I cooked breakfast on my stove and then we walked to Beauly to buy food. Headlines announced 'Russia has The Bomb'. Later we strode out the road, thumbing lifts in vain, and took a bus to Struy. In great heat we walked up the glen road, but thunder clouds soon hid the sun. Many redpolls called in the birches. Five miles up, I grilled kippers on a fire of fallen birch twigs for our lunch.

A shooting tenant's son took us in his car to Deanie Lodge and gave us some venison. He said stalking is poor because hot weather has driven the stags to the high tops. We walked miles to Inchvuilt, where Duncan Fraser's son said we could stay in a bothy at the old lumber camp, but should not go to Monar because the shooting tenant is there. He asked us to keep off the hills because Lord Lovat is at Braulen for stalking, but told us to fish as much as we liked.

Although the bothy windows had holes, unlimited firewood lay outside. I fried venison on the fire. Then we walked to the Garbh-uisge gorge and lay on rocks while fishing the turbulent river till after dark, a beautiful starry night. Fishing was poor because of low water and we caught only two small trout. In the bothy we lay on a single bedstead with a wire floor, very hard in places.

25 September. Glen Strathfarrar

Stewart's roaring laughter woke me at 0200. He was cold and stiff, and saw the irony of lying on the bed's iron rim. Later we awoke to a fine morning. I spotted Duncan Fraser at Inchvuilt, so we walked to see him. He sat in a wheelbarrow while speaking to a gillie and us. "Deer stalking's finished. I've been here 50 years. I remember the day I'd four stalkers under me and a dozen gillies. Now I've one gillie and I'm supposed to look after cattle too. The cattle round-up was a sham, not 650 as reported, but 450, many of them taken from Beauly the day before to swell the total for the press. Lord Lovat did it to try to stop a hydro scheme, but very little pasture would be flooded". A Gaelic speaker who spoke English with a strong Highland accent joined us. When I peeled an orange and offered a piece to him, he said he had never seen one except in pictures.

Stewart and I walked to the rocky Meall an Tairbh for a hazy view of Loch Monar. At the gorge we fished till afternoon, catching a trout, but enjoyed seeing the river foaming over rocks and sparkling in the sun. A robin singing at the bothy had a brown breast with only a spot of red, obviously in moult, and we saw a cock stonechat. In the evening Duncan and family rounded up cattle to much shouting and laughter. Later we watched a red sunset among black clouds beyond Sgurr na Lapaich. A meal and chat by the fire took us to 11. In pitch darkness and thick fog, with no torch we could hardly find our way to the burn for a drink.

26 September. Glen Strathfarrar to Lairig Ghru

Stewart awoke cold at 4 am to light a fire, and when I rose at 5.30 I had never seen such a big fire in a bothy. After eating our last food, we set off at 7 in thick fog, sorry to leave. As we walked quickly down the road, the rocky Sgor na Diollaid rose in red sunshine above the fog. Loch Beannacharan's mirror surface reflected twisting fog spirals where a duck goosander and grey wagtails flew, and mewing buzzards soared. At 8.30 we reached the lumber camp, where an old Fife man who was here on my April trip gave us a great welcome and hot tea. The lorry did not come till much later, but after timber loading we boarded and roared down the glen.

What a morning! The sky was cloudless, the sun warm and the glen in best colour. Birches had turned yellow, and bracken a riot of golden-brown under dark green firs. The steep crags dotted with trees, the river foaming below, the view of Sgurr na Lapaich, the bright blue sky, all made the finest scenery I have ever seen. Standing on the back of the lorry, dodging branches and rushing fast, we came right into Beauly. There we boarded a bus to Inverness, to find all shops closed. At the station we parted. Stewart was to go home and on to Denmark, I to Aviemore.

Soon I stood on a train looking at the golden moors of Slochd and down to Spey. At 6 pm I left Aviemore and despite a 25-lb pack reached the Cairngorm Club footbridge in an hour. Rothiemurchus looked serene and beautiful in evening sunshine. The light failed after I passed the last trees, and from the burn onwards I strained to pick a way, for I had no torch. Near the summit I fell in the dark, so decided to bivouac among boulders. I put on all clothes and crawled into a sleeping bag at 9, but could not sleep. Distant lights shone in Speyside, and above me rose Ben Macdui's skyline and a show of stars. Showers of meteorites shot swiftly, leaving red trails. Breaking the quiet there came an occasional wind eddy, the rush of the March Burn, and sometimes a boulder crashing down screes. For hours I watched stars and the best display of meteorites I had ever seen.

27 September. To Derry Cairngorm

Eventually I slept, and woke slightly cold and stiff as the stars dimmed. Melted frost had wetted the outside of my sleeping bag. In the half light I left at 7, and soon heard cock ptarmigan croaking. A hen sang, jumping off a boulder and fluttering back again while cooing almost like a dog's howl, echoing across the pass. Near the Pools of Dee, cocks strutted with drooped wings and fanned tails, snorting loudly, and a cock chased a hen. I saw two snow patches in Garbh Choire Mor. Many stags roared in Glen Dee, but only one big one, a ten-pointer with 20 hinds. Thin mist hung on the cone of Cairn Toul and the sun turned it to a writhing flame, but the brightness was short-lived, for clouds came with the dawn.

I reached Luibeg at 9, just as Willie Grant arrived. They all got a surprise at seeing me. Bob and Willie went to Derry Cairngorm to shoot ptarmigan, and after breakfast and a rest I followed on an invigorating day of high wind. I felt tired on Carn Crom, but recovered on reaching high ground and walked to the top of Derry Cairngorm where I met Bob. He had shot a hare, but he and Willie got no ptarmigan. Later we saw flocks of 6–20 ptarmigan but never came within 50 yards. Past waterfalls we descended a burn to the foot of the Sron Riach and then home on a lovely evening. Though tired, after a good shandy we spent a fine evening exchanging news.

30 September. To the Scottish Ornithologists Club annual conference in Perth

In the evening at the Conference I met W.B. Alexander the director of the British Trust for Ornithology in Oxford, and James Fisher. James was terribly interested in our trip to Iceland – he flew up with Julian Huxley in June and visited the Westmann Islands to count the gannets. Our Haganes gannet station is a new one to him, also the fulmar colonies in Eyjafjordur.

1 October. SOC Conference, Perth

During a break for coffee in the Black Watch Museum, I had coffee with James. He told me he had phoned Dad in July asking me to go to St Kilda, Sula Sgeir, North Rona and Sule Stack with him, but of course I was in Iceland. He suggests a trip to North-west Greenland next summer to look for fulmars – nobody has been there since Nansen and Peary made observations. He's dead keen and thinks it'll be possible to get a seaplane up and have the Canadian Air Force pay expenses. Prof W-E is keen too. James says "I think we should have a good trip, don't you, Adam?" The prospect is very thrilling anyway. I'll save it up.

15 October. At Aberdeen University

Prof Wynne-Edwards has had an offer to go on an expedition of the Arctic Institute of North America to Baffin Island, lucky man.

Sunday 20 November. Ben Macdui

Last night at Luibeg I saw an aurora. After a late start, Dad and I walked up Glen Luibeg under low cloud, but a brief vista of a glistening Coire Sputan Dearg showed that we might rise into sunshine. After walking up the Sron Riach in fog, at 3700 feet we came out of it to see sunlight blazing on the spotless peak above, and rime sparkling on rocks and snow. A hole in the fog revealed an unusual view into dark Lairig Ghru. Fog engulfed us again, but as we climbed on ski to the Sappers' Bothy we came above it. Nothing could have been finer than the brilliance of sunlit powder snow and hard blue shadows, with dark cloud all around. On skis we raced to the summit as tenuous fog wisps tore past and the sun blazed forth. Over a writhing sea of clouds, Sgor an Lochain Uaine and Braeriach glistened, and beyond them, massive clouds towered into the blue sky. Another view unfolded north over the spotless plateau to Ben Rinnes, a cold blue cone above the clouds. Then fog enveloped us in gloom.

We did some practice skiing on packed powder by the Sappers' Bothy. Then, keeping careful direction, I skied down to the cliff edge, with visibility at five yards. Fast steep swoops in thin fog followed, with a glorious schuss down to and over a frozen lochan. Here for an hour we ran on magnificent powder, but at last left at 4 as snow drifted on a bitter wind and the light thickened.

Fine ski running took us to Loch Etchachan, where we came out of mist and saw boulders hoary with snow and rime. Coire Etchachan in twilight looked gloomy, but the sky began to clear and stars winked. Now there followed a walk in the dark on a wet slippery path. We had to go on hands and knees over ice-covered footbridges. Over-confident at being able to see in the dark, I fell through a hole in the lower bridge and tore a shin. Among the old firs beside the rushing Derry Burn we felt at peace. A late stag roared.

At Luibeg we arrived tired at 7, but after a meal and cups of tea felt elated. Today I saw fox tracks, one at 3000 ft on the Sron Riach, one on the plateau, one below the lochans and one in Coire Etchachan, the last with a limp, obviously the one that escaped recently from one of Bob's traps. We arrived in Aberdeen at 11 after a slippery drive on icy roads, a very hard but fine day.

16 December. To Luibeg

It was a mild sunny morning in Aberdeen. Glad to be finished exams, I enjoyed the bus ride to Braemar, with superb views of Ben Avon spotless down to 3000 feet. Striding out with big pack and skis, I got a lift on a lorry to the Canadian Brig, where I crossed Dee and headed up to the Derry Gate at the foot of Glen Lui. Clouds now hid the sun and I faced a strong wind up Glen Lui. After I arrived, Bob and I drove down to get a hind, but saw none and continued to Willie Grant's house at Linn of Dee. I gave them £15 each in eagle rewards. This year the RSPB paid only £5 for a second successful nest, but Bob and Willie are pleased as Punch. In great form, Willie has shot 15–18 hinds per week. As we drove to Luibeg, a cold wind blew tattered clouds and flying sleet, which by midnight turned to snow.

17 December. At Luibeg

A great change, with an inch of new snow, thick skies and snow falling. Bob went to Braemar by car. In the afternoon came heavy storms with the wind rising and enormous snow plumes racing off the hills. I had wonderful skiing in the wood. Four inches of new snow had fallen and the wind lashed the snow about like fury. Carrying a shovel, I skied down Glen Lui to meet Bob, in case he needed help to get through the rapidly increasing drifts. On return, we put his turkeys under cover. As darkness fell, snow stopped falling, but the wind rose and blew clouds of drift. I skied down Glen Lui to meet Wartle at 10 as arranged. In a very thick night of blowing snow, I saw no sign until he appeared at the Black Brig after 11, a bedraggled figure. On the way back I broke a ski track for him to follow me close, and we arrived at Luibeg after midnight to a roaring fire and cups of tea with Bob and Helen.

18 December. Sgor Mor

Wartle and I skied up Glen Luibeg on a frosty crust. Ben Macdui soared against a blue sky dotted with white cloud, and snow clouds loomed. On powder snow we skied by Creagan nan Gabhar to Sgor Mor. Thin mist swirled below us, and Geldie Lodge and Corrour Bothy were remote black dots. We skied down slopes of magnificent hard-packed powder and then whirled down the hollow between Sgor Mor and Sgor Dubh to the wood above Luibeg, before an exciting run through the wood. All day had been windless and silent, so that we heard burns miles away. The snow that had threatened all day now began to fall ever so slowly and softly.

19 December. Sgor Dubh in storm

We woke to find a gale and heavy sleet, turning to wet snow. I went up Sgor Dubh into 18 inches of new moist snow, and near the skyline it drifted like fury, an absolute inferno with a tearing gale lashing thick clouds of drift. On a slope near the top, the snow showed signs of avalanche, so I plunged down again. It has been an extremely wild day, with one of the strongest gales on the west coast for years, gusting to 100 mph.

20 December. Luibeg to Geldie Lodge

There was little change in the poor weather, though the gale has abated somewhat. Wartle and I had arranged to meet Dad at Coylumbridge tonight and, if not, reach Newtonmore as soon as possible. I deemed it too wild to cross the

Cairngorms to Coylum, so we set off at 11 in a thick snow shower up Sgor Dubh, heading for Kingussie. A stiff climb followed up the steep slope as we sank into snow above our knees at every step, carrying heavy packs and skis beside the track of a small avalanche. On the easier gradient above, the snow was hard, with severe drifting of new powder. The shower cleared briefly in time to give us wonderful views of the Cairngorms, ferocious and grey, half smothered in drift and dark clouds. There followed a ski-run down almost to the White Bridge, tricky skiing from hard on to soft snow.

An eagle chased grouse packs, and the glen was full of hinds wading about in deep heather covered by wet snow. We carried skis to Ruigh nan Clach where we ate a snack just as the sun blazed forth after hail showers. There was a beautiful contrast of wet snow glittering like silver, the greenest grass imaginable, and grim black clouds.

As we slipped on skis and started up the road, the clouds cleared quickly and the snow froze hard. Away far beyond the long open glen, a hill gleamed silver against the blue sky, looking very very far away. The snow became so hard that we had to go up on skins. There was plenty of life about, packs of red grouse about 20 at a time, and the same for flocks of snow buntings. We counted about 700 deer in Glen Geldie, nearly all hinds and calves, many already moving down the glen towards Bynack.

The bleakness of the glen impressed us, a cold blue bowl, now that the clouds had begun piling up again and hiding the sun. When we came in sight of distant Geldie Lodge, a guess that there seemed to be no roof was rather startling, but in closer view this proved to be due to snow lying on the roof.

Up here there had been no thaw and the streams were invisible under deep ice and snow. The whole place lay under an average of at least a foot of snow, and the south-west corner of the lodge, now smashed in by gales, was all battered up with snow that had drifted far inside the Lodge, and there are only two good rooms left, one upstairs and one down. It was ironic to see the row of bells in the kitchen, and the bell in each bedroom. Someone had written on a plaster wall "Capitalism has done this to this place, but Socialism would repair it so that the workers could use it, so what about it?" The writer had forgotten of course that capitalism had built the lodge in the first place and the road.

Stewart at Inchvuilt bothy, Glen Strathfarrar, 25 September 1949

Before turning in we had half a dozen runs up from the Lodge, and they were very fast, glorious swoops on frozen snow. Then we installed ourselves in the big downstairs room, got a fire going in the fireplace, and after a fine meal sat cracking round the fire, "climbing the golden peaks of memory". Wartle said he would not care to go through to the next room for firewood if I weren't there, and he wouldn't even sit at the fire, but would try to fall asleep. Certainly this must be one of the loneliest places in Scotland and the shattered Lodge always has an uncanny atmosphere about it. But then, just after a conversation when Wartle had said "Wouldn't it be strange if a bloke knocked on the door and came in" and I replied "Nobody could get here without skis anyway", there was a loud crash followed by a thud like a heavy boot against the door. My reaction was so sudden that I turned round towards the noise and said "Come in!" There was just a whistle of wind through a broken pane for an answer. We rose to find that a door had fallen in, and this led to much laughter.

At 9 o'clock we went outside, crackling hard snow and frost and a wonderful show of stars dusted across the cloud-free sky. A bout of toffee-making followed, next I melted snow for tomorrow's breakfast and put the pan inside a rucksack near the fire, and then we went outside again at 10 o'clock to have a last look out of doors. A wind had sprung up, and now instead of the calmness of the lonely glen and the steeliness of space were the old elemental powers again. Ragged clouds passed above the hills. An odd snowflake fell lightly on the wind. We put on all our clothes, crawled into our sleeping bags and dropped off to sleep, watching the flickering shadows of the dying fire on the walls.

21 December. Geldie Lodge to Kingussie

Waking at 7.30 in cold half light, we cooked breakfast from inside our sleeping bags. It was fiercely cold, but a good breakfast saw us right for the road and we were ready at 9 o'clock. It was light now and I have never seen such a ghastly array of clouds in my life. The whole sky was filled with gnarled masses of blue-black cloud, tinged with red, yellow and green. Tattered wisps of white hung below them. A remarkable yellowish-green light invested the whole glen and, as we looked, a few snowflakes fell on a rising west wind. It was so forbidding that on its appearance alone, we deliberated whether we should go on or turn back.

I decided for a bash at it, for we could always turn with the wind on our backs if a storm came before we reached the top. Wartle agreed. So we slipped on the skis and swished rapidly to the bridge, then up and down hillocks, for the path lay invisible under deep snow. Many small flocks of snow buntings flew about restlessly, and we must have seen about 300 altogether, as well as plenty of red grouse. A dipper was singing from an iced-up boulder in a tiny clear part of the burn. There must have been over 300 hinds up here in three lots, the lowest lot near the Lodge. Already they were on the move down the glen, in single file. The bottom two lots ran down at a fast trot and the last lot of about 150 stayed until 9.20 and then cleared out, passing the Lodge and still going strongly at 9.45. All this time the wind was rising and snowflakes falling more regularly, and gradually the clouds came lower and hid the Gaick hills beyond the upper Feshie.

We were half a mile from the top when the blizzard came with a rush, obscuring everything as it advanced like a massive grey curtain, then nothing but drift and thick flakes. Near the summit a wren flew out of snow-covered heather beside my skis. We skied down to the river Eidart, and hopped across from boulder to boulder as 20 stags ran down Glen Feshie all out. Down to the Eidart bothy we skied for a breather and a snack. The bothy held much drifted snow and water, but also a good bed with a wire mattress. Out again, we found already an inch of fresh snow and more battering snow falling heavily in a strong wind. For the next few miles Wartle had a lot of trouble, collecting fresh moist snow under his skis, for his were not as well waxed as mine. I left clean tracks for him to follow more easily.

Eventually we came among trees on rocky slopes, wild and spectacular. We had to carry the skis because continuous snow had run out. The steep craggy faces on either side were clothed with firs and half obscured in heavy falling snow. This gave Wartle a grand introduction to the glen. Here it was quiet and sheltered, but higher up the wind blew veils of snow quickly past the crags. We saw many coal tits, an eagle and a buzzard, five ravens, a few bullfinches, and hundreds of stags and hinds on the grassy flats.

After a long way we saw Glenfeshie Lodge, below the freezing level now and here the falling snow was turning to slush. We waded straight through the river Feshie without removing wet boots and socks, and then walked to the Lodge. Here a painter hailed us, a man from Dundee, and asked us in for a cup of tea. He laid out food of many kinds for us and lit a fire, and we ate sandwiches while partly drying our clothes at the fire. A member of a cycling club, he is in charge of a team painting the whole Lodge, and meantime they are bothying in the Lodge. Attempts to phone Dad failed because the gales and snow had brought the lines down, so we had to go on.

As we set off, the sun shone on the firs and Carn Ban Mor shimmered like silk, but it was all short-lived, and darkness came early with heavy clouds and wet snow falling. We decided that the quickest way would be to to dump our kit a few miles down the road and then take the short-cut track to Drumguish, and this we did, for our wet packs and skis were a sore weight by now. There followed a trek across a wild moorland that looked desolate in the murk, and in the middle of the basin the road simply disappeared for half a mile, washed away by floods. We had to cross four big burns in flood, one by combined efforts on a wobbly fence that would have led to complete duckings if we had overbalanced together. Splashing through a bog, we came on to the road again, where we waded about in many drifts of snow. Then we walked down down down, now with electric blue lights shining far off under the blackness of the hills and the night, amid snow showers – Kingussie!

A muddy track through the woods led us to the public road at Drumguish where we got a lift for the last mile. It felt very strange to come into the bright lights of the town on the back of a lorry after what has been a hard but very memorable trek. We phoned Dad at Main's Hotel in Newtonmore, and soon he appeared in his car. He said there was a great blizzard today at Drumochter and at Glen Banchor, so thick that he did not go on the hill. He drove to Main's Hotel, where he took us to a fireside and a beer shandy at the bar, followed by a large hot supper, a fire-lit lounge, and then a warm bedroom with hot-water bottles and other hotel comforts, a different world. The contrast with the last two days seemed ludicrous.

28 December. To the Monadh Liath

After yesterday's starry night with moonlight shimmering silver on Loch Garry, Tom Weir and I woke at Newtonmore to a cold grey morning. Snow began to fall thickly, and continued off and on all day, turning to sleet. We walked up Glen Banchor to visit Glenballoch shepherd Archie Anderson, whose wife asked us in for tea and iced cake while Archie recalled winter experiences as a Lovat Scout in the Canadian Rockies. He told us to use the cottage down the road.

We went out on ski as the sky had cleared. However, a heavy snowstorm swept down quickly, and the skis hardly ran in the sticky snow. Then the falling snow turned to torrential sleet and we retreated to the cottage, soaked to the skin. While Tom lit a stove, I found dry twigs and fallen branches, and blew and coaxed a fire into action. Then we stood side by side with no clothes on for a few minutes, backsides to the fire, to dry our skin before donning dry clothes. Tom cooked a meal while wet clothes steamed at the fire and we discussed life, the universe and religion. Outside was a foul night of rain, with wet snow falling off the roof and splashing on the ground. We cursed Scottish weather.

29 December. Tom Weir's birthday on the Monadh Liath

Today was Tom's 35th birthday. From last night's weather we expected a bad day. Instead, at 7.30 we rose to find crackling frost, I think about 12 F, and not a cloud to dim the sky, with a breathless hush and a fog sea over Spey. We had breakfast of bacon, eggs and tea. About 9 the sky lightened to pale green and the sun suddenly blazed on the hills at the head of the glen. Of a warm rosy hue they stood out against the green of the sky, and though the glen still lay in blue shadow, things were lighting up in all directions. Away to the east the snowy ridges of the Cairngorms gleamed as if on fire, but it was when we strode up the glen carrying our skis that the full beauty of this morning was impressed on us. Now at Dalballoch the whole glen flooded with light that sparkled like diamonds on the snow-covered heather. The red light on the hills had changed to a warm creamy colour, and what a peak ahead was Carn Dearg, a smooth cone of snow sweeping up into the dark blue sky. A tough ascent followed in heather, boulders and deep soft snow to Carn Macoul. There we put on our skis and swooped to the col on magnificent powder snow, and then up Carn Dearg on skins. About 80 ptarmigan rushed past in tight packs, and one pure white bird flashed close above us against the blue sky. Now we saw why they had flown, as a pair of eagles sailed past the cornice edge quite close, warm and golden in the sun.

Towards the top of Carn Dearg I skied ahead fast, eager for the view. Yesterday's storm never touched Dalwhinnie or the Cairngorms, but plastered the Monadh Liath, Creag Meagaidh and the north-west Highlands. Black and silver clouds hung over Ben Alder and swamped Creag Meagaidh, but elsewhere the sun blazed from deep blue sky. To the north-west, peaks from Knoydart to Ben Wyvis shone creamy in the sun, their corries blue in the shadow. They looked like polar hills, utterly remote and cold. Nearer lay Loch Dubh below a wild corrie, and all the way along on our right a corniced drop into Gleann Ballach.

Now we skied down and up to another top, and down and up again to Carn Ban, with magnificent skiing in windless air and wonderful powder snow, the finest I have ever seen apart from New Year 1949 in Glen Luibeg. Fast glorious runs followed from Carn Ban over wave-like humps that sent us airborne, great fun flying through the air to land with a loud slap and then swish on again. A long gradual climb followed to Carn Ballach with a few short downhill runs on the way. In top form, I had gone well ahead and out of sight of Tom, who is not in form yet after his flu. As I swished gently into a snowy bowl, I looked at my shadow flying a long way over the slope, and at my ski tracks twisting far behind, two parallel lines of blue in a silver world.

It was cold as I waited ten minutes for Tom. What a place this would be in a blizzard, with snowy plateaux for many miles. The light had turned mellow, with the Cairngorms mauve coloured save for the silvery blue of the high plateaux. Then Tom appeared, a toiling black speck ¼ mile away, adding to the vastness of the Monadh Liath. For a time our atheism of last night took a back seat. The world was so intensely beautiful that I could scarcely grasp it all. I can still catch some impressions, but adequate description is beyond me. Together we marvelled at its loveliness, and Tom said it was the finest birthday present he could ever have wished.

Now on with the skis again, and we swooped out of the sun over velvety snowfields. Fast traverses followed down the east side of Meall na Ceardaich and some glorious long runs into the glen. There we sat by the burn for a while and watched the last of the sun dying on the corniced ridges high on Carn Dearg. Down Allt Fionndrigh we put on skis again, rattling down hard frozen snow in great style right to the cottage door. I searched for fallen branches and made a blazing fire while Tom cooked. A memorable meal followed. Our chief talk was of today's tour. Somehow the views and impressions were so numerous and ever-changing that we found it hard to re-live them again in conversation. We seemed to have done and seen such a tremendous lot in the space of six hours. It has been one of the finest days of my life.

30 December. Skiing on A' Chailleach

Thaw, a gloomy morning with rain and the lower hills quite black, an amazing transformation from yesterday evening's 6–8 inches of snow, frost and cloudless sky. But we set off and carried skis up the steep Creag na h-Iolaire, an unrelenting slope where the skis seemed massive weights as we sweated in humid air. At the top we had a snack and marvelled at the awe-inspiring mass of clouds rolling up from the south. Three ravens flew over croaking loudly, adding to the impression of a world of mystery and darkness about to end the next minute.

We skied down a short way and then two miles up to A' Chailleach, where a gale blew. It was freezing, and the cairn carried frozen fog crystals. Our impressions were of a grim planet about to suffer catastrophe. Under black clouds pouring over Carn Dearg, the snow looked dirty grey, and shafts of light poked through oily-looking cloud, tracing patches of lurid orange on the snow. Black and yellow clouds loomed through grey haze. We expected a storm, but none came.

Frozen snow gave a fine run off the summit, but sticky snow a poor main run to the red bothy, apart from the last part down the burn, fast and quite exciting. At the cottage we had a meal, and then, sorry to leave, walked to Newtonmore to meet climbing pals from the Scottish Mountaineering Club up from Glasgow for the New Year. Mist and sleet for the next few days brought home to Tom and me how lucky we had been on his birthday.

Chapter 10. Early 1950

2 April. To Corrour Bothy at night

A wild day of wind arrived, with heavy snow showers. I intended to go to Corrour and waited till evening, hoping for a clearance. None came, so I left anyway, astounded as four cyclists arrived from Aviemore, wearing cycle shoes, ankle socks and shorts.

Bob and Dad accompanied me to the new footbridge in Glen Luibeg. By now dusk had come, under a gloomy sky. The snow stopped falling, but near the shoulder of Carn a' Mhaim a blizzard struck, driving in my face, so I had a real struggle. Came a clearance with wild clouds tearing across the sky, a few stars and the Devil's Point looming, but then the storm was on again, battering like mad. The Devil's Point was my mark for knowing when to leave the path, but now I could see no more than a few feet. I plodded down to Dee, but did not recognise the place. The torchlight accentuated the blinding white wall of flakes in front, but I shone it on a spot where the water seemed to run a few inches above shingle and plunged in. Immediately I realised I had not been careful enough with the torch, for the water came to my knees. I carried on, up to the lower thighs, to stagger out on the far bank with a heavy pack as well as cold legs and feet.

I set a compass course north-west for Allt a' Choire Odhair and walked 300 yards before realising I must be north of the burn, so then set a course south, in pitch darkness and heavy snowfall. At last I reached the burn and knew I would soon be at the bothy. Then I saw a light. Someone outside for a pee had seen my light and flashed his torch in return. Shortly I came inside, trying to see through smoke. Aberdeen student Barney is here with two pals. Yesterday's wet snow soaked them, so they lay in sleeping-bags all day today. I put on dry trousers and socks, and with Barney's tea inside me I felt a new man. Snow drifted through holes in the roof, but later went off and by 10 the clouds had cleared, though a tearing gale still battered the bothy and whirled the drifting snow outside. A full moon shone. They told of a total eclipse at 9. I arrived at 9.40, which explains the pitch darkness. Bedding down close together, we soon fell asleep.

3 April. On Cairn Toul

I awoke to find a north-west gale and snow showers, with some spells of blazing sunshine. Folk in the bothy left for Aviemore. The Devil's Point looked colossal, trailing snow plumes into blue sky. Snow buntings twittered outside the bothy and a golden eagle soared far above. In the afternoon I had fine skiing in the Coire Odhar on beautiful powder snow, and found ptarmigan pairs numerous. On skis I climbed to the Slichit but found no ptarmigan high up, not surprising because of the deep snow and tearing drift. Sudden fierce storms came on a high wind, dying a bit at night. This Corrour is a grand place. The noise of the wind is for music.

4 April. To Sgor an Lochain Uaine in dense mist

I decided to go through to Speyside today, as it was perfectly calm and frosty, with wonderful sunshine. I left with full kit and skis in great spirits, but noticed thick haze spreading from the south-west. By the time I skied to the top of Coire Odhar, wild clouds filled the sky. I skied quickly, reaching Cairn Toul at 12.30, but dense mist cut visibility to eight yards. Once I saw through a hole in the clouds into a ghastly chasm, with the snow a filthy grey colour in the gloomy light. Past Sgor an Lochain Uaine I continued in the mist, but turned at the col above the Garbh Choire Mor because visibility fell to four yards and flakes of snow whirled past. It would be almost impossible to see the edge of the huge cornices that I knew ringed the Garbh Choire Mor.

A tiring return followed. On the snow, I could see no further than my ski tips. I did not know if I was going up or down, and fell at each unseen bump. The 1000-foot run off Cairn Toul, where I had flashed uphill in the sun, seemed endlessly slow and strenuous, with dozens of falls and leg strains. At last, in thickening snowfall I emerged from mist at the top of Coire Odhar. I had a welcome sitting glissade for 250 feet of height, followed by a ski-run for more than that, and then a walk in thick falling snow. Now that I stood at the bothy and required no further concentration and willpower, I suddenly felt very tired, but recovered once I had dropped my pack.

With the wind round to the south, mist to 2500 feet and wet falling snow, the outlook was dismal. However, I carried up dry sticks two days ago and lit a fire to dry clothes and cook a meal. A man dripping wet came in after carrying skis from Glen More over the Lairig. After much blowing of embers we had a fire and good conversation.

5 April. Ben Macdui

It was a fine sunny morning. I decided to go to Luibeg for mail, via Ben Macdui. I left much kit at Corrour Bothy and walked up the Lairig Ghru, meeting a lame poorly clad exhausted man who had left Aviemore at 0400. Later I heard he reached Luibeg at 4 pm, quite crazy. Deep snow lay above 2500 feet. On the exposed ridge south-west of the summit the slippery snow-covered boulders made climbing slow and trying. At the summit came wild views, but long ere now the clouds had lowered from the west and a blizzard of hail swept down. Slipping on the skis, I reached Loch Etchachan in ten minutes after a wonderful run on powder snow all the way. Gloom now pervaded everything and mists covered the hills. I skied on to Derry Cairngorm on sastrugis with deep troughs, and fell twice, straining legs and skis. At Luibeg I read a letter from Tom Weir who hopes to see me in Speyside and leaves soon for the Himalaya.

6 April. Ben Macdui

Carrying a fair load, I left for Speyside on a lovely cloudless frosty morning, but climbed Sron Riach in rapidly worsening weather that soon brought thick mist. As I climbed to 4000 feet I got a slight scare at the huge cornices, which merged too well with the mist. Leaving the skis I returned on foot, sure of a thaw coming. I arrived at 2 pm with the mist down to 2000 feet. Bob and I went up Glen Derry and had fine views of a cock capercaillie and many crossbills. We walked round his traps, getting a fox. Ian and Allan McNicol arrived from Glen More. Miss A. Sheriffs from Glasgow, staying at Luibeg, amused us with tales of her fears in the hills. I have never seen anyone who talked so much. Ian, Allan and I decided to go to Speyside rain or shine tomorrow.

7 April. Luibeg to Glen More

Morning dawned with mist at 2500 feet, a gale and heavy rain. The McNicols walked by Glen Derry and Strath Nethy. First I had to go to 4000 feet for my skis. A big thaw had come, with lashing sleet even at the top. Poor skiing on sticky snow followed for 1000 feet and a slippery walk into the Lairig Ghru, where I left my skis. Now I waded Dee to Corrour to collect my kit, waded back, and walked to my skis. Rain lashed from the south-west. A gale roared at the Lairig summit, helping me along, and below Creag a' Chalamain I crossed slippery boulders in torrential rain with the gale at my back. I arrived at the McNicol's camp absolutely soaked to the skin at 6.30, a few minutes after the McNicols, but we soon cooked a fine meal. I have rarely seen a worse day, and the mild air has melted much snow. Rain still lashed down at night, though turning colder.

8 April. Downhill skiing in Coire Cas

After a good sleep, I woke to find the tops white, a south-west gale, and heavy sleet showers. The McNicols can camp on condition that they light no fire, so we had to put on wet socks and clothes. We walked to Coire Cas, where many skiers had gathered. Three inches of fresh snow had fallen. A long drift lay on Allt a' Choire Chais. I saw many good downhill skiers, Ian being one of them. It became dangerous towards late afternoon due to congestion from too many folk.

We walked to camp. The others got a lift to the Dell Hotel, but I stayed, expecting Tom Weir. After a good meal, I lay in my sleeping bag with the tent door partly open, watching snow falling and listening to a gale in the trees, snow pattering on the tent, and the roar of the Allt Mor. To dry my wet socks I wear one pair dry with two wet pairs on top, inside the sleeping bag. The wet ones are merely damp next morning. After a last cup of tea I went early to bed.

9 April. More downhill skiing in Coire Cas

An inch of snow lay and fresh snow whitened the tops, again with a south-west wind and murky clouds, but a cheerier morning. Crested tits sang outside the tent, and a mistle thrush, dunnock, coal tit and chaffinch, a nice chorus. The McNicols arrived, speaking of hot baths and dry clothes. My wet trousers and damp socks began to dry as I walked uphill.

We carried skis to Coire Cas where a short-lived sunny blink appeared. On skins we climbed to the summit and skied fast down Coire na Ciste. Despite frequent thick showers all day, the organisers decided to hold races but kept us waiting for hours until starting at 4.30. They ran an exciting race in a snowstorm and we saw some good skiing. Homewards we skied by the wide hollow on the east side of Coire Cas in a blizzard, eyes painful with gale-blown drift.

Cairn Gorm from Derry Cairngorm, 13 May 1950

A racer gave us a lift in his car to the Dell Hotel, where I donned Ian's spare clothes and we dined before going by van to Aviemore Hotel. There we gate-crashed but nobody noticed in the half-dark amid cigar smoke and dinner jackets. The films showed the latest downhill technique. In a blizzard we drove to the Dell. I spread my sleeping bag in a hut where a wind howled through open windows, so I covered the gaps with boards. At midnight, a car barged in with two men who laughed uproariously at suddenly finding a sleeping person.

10 April. Coire Cas and Clach Bharraig Bothy

On a grey morning I made breakfast in the hut, chatted with the farmer, and then hitched a lift to Glenmore Lodge, but saw no sign of Tom. Three inches of snow lay at Glen More, and peewits and a greenshank fed at Loch Morlich. We walked to Coire Cas to ski and found deep snow. Today I broke both cane sticks in a fall, and going to Luibeg without them will be harder. The McNicols left a lot of unused food for me at their camp site and then headed for Glasgow. In the evening I walked to Clach Bharraig bothy, where a Lomond Club man and a Birmingham teacher had a fire in one corner, so I dried my clothes and cooked a meal on the fire. Good conversation and so to bed.

11 April. Clach Bharraig to Luibeg

I rose to a better morning, and so decided to go to Luibeg, as the weather has been unsuitable for this for nearly a week. An inch of fresh snow lay, and a dipper and wren sang. I left at 10 with a heavy pack. A long heavy plod followed up to the bottom of the big snow-filled gully running down Allt Creag an Leth-choin, through long heather with three inches of fresh snow to start with and six to eight inches to finish, but not enough for skiing. Up the gully I went on skins, wind getting up and already big cloud barriers building over the Monadh Liath. Drifting snow was tearing about, so I battered on at full speed with skins off and sliding over the Miadan at a good spin. By now, clouds were coming down everywhere and odd flakes tore past. The views of Sgoran Dubh and Sron na Lairige were among the grimmest I have ever seen.

Away westward, Creag Meagaidh and the Laggan Bridge hills, spotlessly white, were being engulfed in storm. Mist settled on Cairn Lochan, so I pushed on, never felt so fit, just time to reach the top of the Lochan Buidhe and see my way ahead before the mist closed in. I skimmed down to there from Cairn Lochan in a minute or two over long velvety drifts, then in the mist a long gradual pull up a broad snowfield, out of the mist and up to the North Top by slopes of old snow, so hard that my soles were slipping dangerously, and a run off the North Top to the col at great speed over icy snow, though rather frightening. I was on the summit at 1.10 pm, three hours and ten minutes from Clach Bharraig, with only one rest of five minutes below the North Top. Storm was closing in all over Scotland, and there were grim views of black, grey and white clouds lowering on the hills. I left in a short furious blizzard and skied quickly to Loch Etchachan, a beautiful fast run, then down Coire Etchachan almost to the Derry crossing, wonderful snow all the way.

It was queer to be in Glen Derry and see green grass in a burst of sunlight, and sit sunbathing a while by the Glas Allt Mor, it was all too good. I watched 200 hinds and calves grazing. Blue sky, sparkling snow and blue shadows, a big hailstorm and then a long clear spell as I reached Luibeg. The tops Beinn Bhrotain and the Monadh Mor shone with silver against the dark sky, the evening light was intense and sharp on the snowy hills, on the old pines, and on the incredible blue of the burn. A pair of oystercatchers 'kleeped' joyously from the grassy flats and a cock crossbill sang close up near the lodge, burning red in the sun. What a kick one gets out of life at times, experiences so intense that a thrill of sheer joy runs all over one. Tired but happy, I arrived at Luibeg. It was snowing tonight.

13 April. At Luibeg

A north wind blew, with grey sky and an inch of snow. Bob and I logged in the forenoon, and went down Glen Lui in the afternoon after roe, but saw only two far out. In a distant glen we visited an eyrie that was occupied earlier, but snow filled it today, so we fear she has been robbed.

14 April. On Ben Macdui

My 20th birthday, but I forgot till evening. With skis I left for Ben Macdui despite heavy snow showers. I climbed on skins from 2200 feet to the summit and have hardly ever seen these hills so white. Bursts of sun peeped through but gradually it became gloomier, and at the tor on the Sron Riach the finest of flakes fell in beautiful crystals with extraordinary patterns, mostly star-like.

Making tea above Loch Etchachan, AW sen, Sandy Russell, Jock Topp, 13 May 1950

Thick mist hid the top above Coire an Lochain Uaine, but lifted as I reached it. I swept down to Loch Etchachan on a thrilling fast run over powder, marred slightly by fairly poor visibility. I skied right on to the loch, where deep snow covered the edge. In dead calm air I clearly heard my heart beating and drumming sounds in my ears.

The sun appeared, so I climbed on skins to the plateau again and swooped to Loch Etchachan on magnificent snow. I have never seen such good skiing, absolutely breathtaking. I skied all the way to Carn Crom, with great runs on Derry Cairngorm and below it on hard-packed velvety powder snow. After skiing there for half an hour which improved my turns, I walked down to Luibeg, elated by a wonderful day. Dad and Mum arrived tonight and also Sandy Russell.

15 April. Derry Cairngorm and Ben Macdui

A beautiful dawn came with frost, cloudless skies and wonderful colours. Sandy, Dad and I carried skis to Carn Crom and then skied to Derry Cairngorm and Ben Macdui, seeing Arctic-like views with hills shining white against a deep blue sky. From the summit we swooped into the Snowy Corrie, with jumps at the bottom on hard ridges. It was so good that we returned for a second swoop.

Clouds now came in and a rising wind turned cold, so we climbed to the top above Coire Sputan Dearg for the last time. A long run led to Loch Etchachan, and I took it as fast as I have ever done, on perfect powder and with a couple of natural jumps on the way.

Near the loch we met Jock Topp and a friend who had also been skiing. Sandy and I had carried up some dead pine branches and now lit a fire in a patch of boulders. We boiled a pot of water for tea. While sitting to eat a snack, we heard a screaming rush and turned to see a golden eagle 50 feet up, swooping with half-closed wings after a cock ptarmigan. The cock ptarmigan flew straight to us and crouched nearby, obviously to avoid the eagle. The eagle came to 20 feet in a headlong rush before seeing us and flying out of sight. On frozen snow we skied fast down Coire Etchachan.

27 April, 1960. At Aberdeen University

I had a long chat at Marischal College with Prof Wynne-Edwards about my ptarmigan study, and he suggests it as an Honours subject. We have picked Derry Cairngorm as the main study area. The Prof leaves for Baffin Island on Monday (1 May).

5 May. To camp on Carn Crom

In the afternoon I went from Aberdeen to Ballater by bus and then cycled to Luibeg, on a lovely warm day with white fleecy clouds, hills sharp and clear, and the woods bursting with life. Many willow warblers sang, some tree pipits, a redstart, and at Inverey a cuckoo, but a cuckoo has not yet called at Luibeg. Evening colours were spectacular on the trees, the sparkling burn and the gold flush on the hills. Carrying tent and skis, I left at 9.45 as frost began to grip, to pitch camp near Carn Crom summit. It was a wonderful night, with waves of dark silent hills velvety black against a sky beginning to glitter with stars, and the sound of burns high with snow water.

6 May. On Ben Macdui

I woke at 4 am to find dense mist. At 6 I woke again, now just above the mist, with clouds breaking up all around. Later the sun rose above the clouds and for a second turned a thin wraith of cloud over Glen Derry into a flame. The high tops burned warmly in the alpenglow of dawn, thrusting above blue-grey and creamy clouds. They still carried much snow, the highest parts of Braeriach and Ben Macdui being almost spotless. Avalanches had fallen in Coire Sputan Dearg but big cornices still stand intact without a crack. After carrying skis to Derry Cairngorm, I skied to Ben Macdui and had an exhilarating run towards Loch Etchachan. Off Derry Cairngorm I had a straight run down east of Little Cairngorm to the col short of Carn Crom. Leaving tent, skis and other equipment, I descended to Luibeg in worsening weather with mist and rain. I accompanied Bob as he drove Helen Scott to Braemar to take a bus to Aberdeen for a few days, and returned with him to "bothy in the hoose".

12 May. To Carn Crom camp

This weekend I had intended to study for exams, but the weather was too good and Dad said he would go to the Cairngorms, so I went too. Sandy Findlater, a medical student in my digs, has wanted to go for some time and has bought skis, and today I asked him. After tea, we left in his car. In Aberdeen I spotted Sandy Russell and we gave him a lift. Deeside was looking absolutely magnificent, and we saw a fine great spotted woodpecker in birches west of Braemar. Sandy, Dad, David Britten a friend of Dad's, and I set off up Carn Crom at 10.45. We erected a second tent beside my standing one. Before going to bed I had a few ski runs on a snowfield below the tent, on snow already frozen hard with the night frost.

13 May. On Ben Macdui

At 5 we woke to find a dream of a morning. Lochnagar and all the hills to the south had a soft blue colour, above parallel sheets of cloud lit by golden sunlight. Sandy and I strolled and then wakened Dad and David before cooking a regal breakfast. On the snowfield, a uniform surface just starting to thaw lay above hard snow, good for giving Sandy his first ski lessons. Then we left for Derry Cairngorm and Ben Macdui, carrying skis in increasingly warm air. At the wee lochan we stopped for a rest, a lovely spot like a miniature glacial lake with the snow 'calving' in blocks. The ice on Loch Etchachan had broken into floes and a huge amount of snow lay on the high tops. Vast numbers of insects lay stranded on the snow at 4000 feet, mostly comatose.

At the summit we had a good view to Mam Sodhail, Creag Meagaidh and Ben Nevis, still well plastered in snow. Sandy Russell and Jock Topp came up, and then we skied into the Snowy Corrie. Later, Sandy, Jock and I ran straight off the North Top into the corrie, a very exciting run with a steep slope at first, finally easing down to the lochans at the north end. There we lazed a while, listening to a snow bunting, and slept. We awoke to eat bradies and drink lime juice, and then climbed for more runs, which became faster in the late afternoon under a beautiful blue sky studded with puffs of cotton-wool cloud. Then we made a last climb on ski to the summit, before a run to the blue lochan by the top of Sputan Dearg, and another swoop to the col above Loch Etchachan. After skiing to Derry Cairngorm we had a fast schuss from the top on rapidly freezing snow to below Little Cairngorm, and then carried our skis over Carn Crom at 8 pm as the sun set in a flood of orange colour over Braeriach plateau.

With sticks carried up last night I made a fire and cooked a meal, followed by tea. Tonight before turning in I walked to Carn Crom summit for a last view, nothing but the thunder of the burns and the emptiness of star-studded space. I recalled the first time I climbed Carn Crom alone in 1943, a great adventure then.

14 May. At Carn Crom camp

I woke early to see thick mist, slept again, and woke at 9 to cook a breakfast of bacon and eggs with tea. With the mist staying dense, the hard snow had thawed slightly, giving very good conditions for skiing on the snowfield below our camp. Sandy and David managed to do crude stem turns. In the afternoon, still in mist, we packed up everything and descended to Derry Lodge. Up Glen Derry we saw a cuckoo, a redstart, a willow warbler, a drake goosander, a woodcock, and a flock of crossbills. Jock Topp had had an accident on Ben Macdui. Side-slipping on skis down a steep narrow gully, he overbalanced when he stopped and somersaulted into boulders, hurting his pelvis on both sides and cracking a ski.

16 October. Glen Quoich

Bob, Dad and I drove down Glen Lui and walked through Clais Fhearnaig. We watched a stag with 40 hinds and a stag with 20 lower down the hill. The hinds tended to move uphill, and soon the upper stag had rounded up the topmost hinds from the lower group. At this the lower stag ran uphill, roaring, and the two stags fought with clashing antlers for at least one and a half minutes. The lower stag withdrew, shaking his head and rubbing one side of his head on a foreleg, and then I spotted a little fresh blood on his head. Now he stopped roaring, while the upper stag rounded up the 60 and moved uphill, trying to mate with different hinds. In the Dubh Ghleann we made a fire and drummed up tea, and then stalked a roe buck, but it saw us and ran off. We returned over Meall an Lundain to the car and then to Luibeg.

On the way to Aberdeen, Dad and I called at Linn of Dee, where Willie Grant showed us a magnificent dog fox, 49 inches nose to tail, that he shot today. In the Garbh Allt wood it looked so big that he mistook it for a roe. When he saw it was a fox he fired his .303 rifle, although it was running over 200 yards away. The bullet shattered its left foreleg and broke its right hind leg, almost severing the hind foot and ankle apart from a thin bit of skin. The fox stopped, barked, and snarled, before running downhill, occasionally raising the shattered foreleg and holding it in its mouth, and amazingly putting a piece of soft wood on the stump hind leg. A few times it stopped to lick its hind leg and snarl. Eventually the hind foot kept tripping it up in tall heather, and it lay down exhausted, whereupon Willie ran to shoot it.

Chapter 11. Lapland and Lofoten 1950

31 May. Planning a summer expedition

I spent the evening at Wartle's (Bert Shepherd's) digs, planning a summer trip. I have given up Spitsbergen, not having heard further from Brian Roberts of the Scott Polar Research Institute. Norway or Iceland are obvious places if all else fails. Jon Sigurgeirsson of Akureyri sent a letter dated 24 April, telling of blizzards and rivers still frozen over. Wartle and I decided to try to get to northern Russia, a big step but well worth the risk I think. Couldn't get to sleep tonight, thinking of it.

AW at hide near eagle nest, 11 June 1950 (photo Robert Carrick)

19 June. More planning

I spent the evening with Wartle discussing plans. Brian Roberts' letter has arrived. We had offered to work a month in Spitsbergen coal mines, so as to get transport on a coal-ship. However, he says the company will take us only if we work a whole season. Obviously it is now too late for a summer trip there this year. We plan to work in the mines for a winter there and then use the spring and summer for ski journeys and later zoological work after the thaw. This summer, Wartle has to attend a potato inspector's course at Edinburgh until late July. Pat Sellar hopes to go to Iceland but must be back here by the third week of July. Wartle and I had hoped to go to north Russia, but we haven't time to plan it now and do not have enough money to go there. Last week we saw a film on an Oxford University expedition to Jan Mayen, a tremendous place too.

23 June. Decision on north Norway

Wartle and I met at the university. Pat has flu, so is unable to go to Iceland till later, maybe not at all. I decided to go alone to Finnmark, next by rail from Narvik into Swedish Lapland, and then to Lofoten to climb. Glasgow climber Allan McNicol advised me to contact Mr Mosbye who runs BP's main oil depot on Lofoten. His daughter Kirsti had spent a year in Glasgow, where Allan knew her, and Allan said she was about to return home. She had told Allan that she knew the local Lofoten climbers and suggested that I meet them. Later I hope to go by fishing boat from Norway to Iceland, to join Jon Sigurgeirsson for a trip to Vatnajökull. Wartle said he hoped to join us there. Our last greetings were "See you in Akureyri in August".

For the trip I had a Bartholomew's map of Scandinavia and Finland, at a scale of 1:2.5 million. I hitch-hiked from East Lothian to Newcastle and then by boat to Bergen and the coastal boat for six days to Kirkenes. Then I walked, took buses and camped across Finnmark to Narvik, and then by rail to camp at Abisko in Swedish Lapland. Next I took the train back to Narvik and by boat to Lofoten. Diary entries for a July climb in Swedish Lapland and an ascent of the highest rock peak in Lofoten with Norwegian mountaineers on 22 July are in my book *It's a fine day for the hill.*

23 July. Feasting below Higravstind

Up at 9 under sun and blue sky, we had breakfast and spent the forenoon lying at ease, drinking coffee and eating cakes. The stove was hardly ever out, always a new brew on the go. We did some jumping and running, but always subsided to coffee. At noon we walked to the village in a shade temperature of 23°C, too hot to climb. We saw that the glacier route off Higravstind is feasible, and then returned to camp.

There Magnar surprised me by announcing we would now have middag (midday meal), though everybody must already be satisfied. It was fantastic, with masses of potatoes, peas and meat of different kinds, stews, and sausage. Emil gave me a big lump of 'blod' or blood pudding and asked if I knew what it was. He said "Eat it first and we'll tell you" and then added "There's a lot of it in Korea just now with the war", but I could see it was black pudding like ours in Scotland. After this we had coffee and cakes, and then a woman from the village, a friend of the climbers, came with a basket of cake and a big jar of sweetened whipped cream mixed with rhubarb. It was so good that we managed to eat all of it.

Then we walked to a boat crowded stiff with everyone from a baby to a grandmother who had to be lifted from the quay to the boat because of a low tide. A fine journey followed in brilliant sun. We sang songs and ate the last chocolate and raisins. They are grand folk and these will be two long-remembered days for me.

24 July. Climbing at Svolvær

Today there was a light east wind. I decided to go to Svolværgeita (Svolvær goat), first walking to a kirk nestling among boulders, birches and rowans at the foot, where blaeberries and crowberries bloomed ripe and shiny on sunny banks. I climbed in shirt, trousers and gym shoes, for at 10.00 the temperature was already 23°C.

After a steep climb through the wood, I came into a broad corrie with scrub birch. Here redpolls, willow warblers and meadow pipits abounded, and some fed fledglings. Birch scrub grows to 1200 feet. I climbed to Svolværgeita, a huge pinnacle of smooth rock with a big drop on the town side and a double horn on top.

I climbed to the back of the pinnacle on slabs and steep grass. Once I had a small fright when a gym shoe began to slip on steep grass above a drop of several hundred feet. I quickly became secure by testing the turf more carefully and climbing a step at a time until reaching easier ground. From a col I had a fine view to Svolvaer on its islands. The ridge was interesting. One place I considered too risky, a traverse along a sheer wall on a crack with an overhang below. Avoiding it by descending a rocky gully, I climbed to the summit of Floya. An airy top giving a brilliant panorama of mountain and sea in hot sunshine, it stood far above Svolvaergeita.

A deep blue sea rippled golden and silver in the sun. Some rock peaks gleamed whitish and others reddish, and Store Molla black, framed in the sea. West lay an inky blue lake with white icebergs floating like huge swans. Further south, Vaagekalentind dominated the skyline, a great rock pyramid. Colours were as rich as I have ever seen.

I went west to 'devil's gate'. On its north side I looked down 2000 feet through a big gap bridged by a rock bar, to a blue lake among birches. A funnel wind blew strongly, and black cliffs glistened with water. Two ravens and a cock ring ouzel flew past. I walked to frog peak, a grey rocky hill like a sitting frog complete with eyes and head.

After bathing in a pool I descended, seeing a few wheatears. In the wood I ate blaeberries, saw some fieldfares, and returned to the Mosbye house at 15.00 after a fine climb. It was 25°C in the shade but someone said 28°C in the town centre.

Honningsvaag rebuilding after German army's scorched earth, July 1950

Snow patch at sea level near Nordkapp, July 1950

25 July. Leaving Lofoten

At Svolvaer on 25 July I boarded *Finnmarken*, one of the Hurtigrute (fast route) ships. It left at 23.00 in heavy rain, with mist on the peaks. Vaagekallentind was spectacular, a vast black triangle of rock rising into a huge white cloud shaped like a saucer, which made it look double its usual height. I met a 17 year-old plasterer Harry Parti, returning to Stavanger after a holiday on the cheap like me. He speaks a little English and is keen to learn more. He had a sleeping bag for use on deck, but heavy rain put this out of the question. I suggested we half-erect my waterproof tent on top of a cargo-hole cover and sleep under the tent, and with a laugh he agreed. Rain battered down and the wind howled around us, but we were warm, although damp. Later we found a better place, two chairs in a warm spot in a corridor beside the engine. Lofoten had retreated in rainy haze, looking more mystical than ever across a grey sea and with the rock-peaks steaming up into the clouds.

26 July. South

This was a day of continuous rain and low cloud almost to sea level, so the journey seemed unending. Using food still left in my rucksack, I cooked meals on my stove under cover in the stern, where we could get hot drinking water easily. For washing up I used boiling water from a steam winch, merely turning the tap on. Harry decided in return to buy all new food at towns where the boat stopped for an hour or more, and today he bought a lump of bacon, bread, milk and oatmeal for porridge. Our meals were crude but fine, and at each meal we attracted the attention of many bored passengers who stood and watched.

Harry whistles at every girl who passes and told me "It's the only ting I tink about. I am very much ashamed". He spends much time singing, and taught me the song Niedelvens about the river in Trondheim, a song that always brings me back to the top of Higravstind, where Emil Olsen and his girl friend sang it as we watched the night sun.

27 July. Trondheim

The boat berthed at Trondheim at 0800 and stayed 12 hours. Rain poured the whole time. Harry and I walked round town and visited the big kirk. On the boat we have a fine place outside but out of the rain, and cooked our meals there. Harry has now necked three girls. A dismal wet evening as we left, and no sleep because of noise and disturbance from overcrowded passengers.

28 July. To Aalesund

Into Molde we came this morning, with rain falling hard and low cloud. At noon we reached Aalesund. By now Harry has necked five girls and still whistles at every girl passing. We cooked meals again, drawing the inevitable crowd. In Aalesund we went ashore and Harry kindly acted as interpreter. Mr Mosbye had said Aalesund is the best place for a fishing boat to Iceland.

28 July. At Aalesund

The harbour-master spoke in Norwegian, which I translate below. He gave exciting news: "A boat leaves for Iceland tonight, the *Staursund*. Come back in an hour". When I returned, he said "Now I am not sure it will land in Iceland, and there will be no other boats for some time". As my spirits ebbed, he added "Wait a moment while I phone the captain". He said "Good news. He will take you tonight. He will not land in Iceland, but will put you on board the first Icelandic boat he meets". I felt like dancing with joy.

Shortly the *Staursund* arrived, a green boat in size between a trawler and a drifter. In the crew's quarters in the foc'sle a spare bunk was in the bows. After walking to a cafe with a magnificent view of the town, I boarded and went to sleep in pitch darkness with the roof two inches above my head. I thought I would waken to see open sea.

29 July. Leaving Aalesund on a Norwegian herring boat

In the morning I awoke, surprised at the quiet and the lack of movement. I looked out and saw Aalesund harbour! The crew had been drunk the night before, hence the delay. We left in early afternoon, just as a big ship came in, but the *Staursund* stole the show with loud bells and horn hooting, and the crew waving mats and shouting. All were drunk. In the foc'sle the crew

Soviet war memorial near Kirkenes, July 1950

Cod drying near Kirkenes

Road-man and son west of Kirkenes, July 1950

Higravtind at midnight, 22 July 1950

Trollvand from Higravtind, 22 July 1950

Geitgaljartind from Higravtind, Rulten sharp peak on left, 22 July 1950

had started a party with six bottles of Norwegian fin (fine) spirit and rum. They gave me great welcome, though I turned down their repeated generous offers of drink.

As we left the fjord, the sea became rough and several tipsy crewmen vomited. A tall lanky man said to me on deck "You, Engelskman (Englishman), you good seaman?" to which I replied "Nei". "Nei?" he said. "Me", he continued, pointing to his stomach, "fucking good seaman", and "Him", pointing to another man, "fucking good seaman". In a friendly tussle, the lanky one knocked the other's cap off and the strong wind blew it into the sea. I said "Me Skotsk, ikke Engelskman" (Scottish, not English man), to which they both shouted "Ja, ikke Engelskman, fin" (Yes, not Englishman, fine).

In the distance I saw the sea-bird cliff of Rundøy. As we headed west the swell increased but I felt fine. At 22.00 the sea became very rough, blue sky had gone and Norway had vanished hours ago. I felt better after vomiting, but had a poor night. The sideways roll was huge. Because my berth had been built across the boat and not along one side, my head was above my feet one moment and vice versa the next.

30 July. Storm off Faeroe

The storm was bad in the early morning, for a strong crosswind blew under low cloud and squally rainstorms. The seas seemed mountainous and big waves often swamped the deck. Used to this, the crew danced along, occasionally clutching a rope as they walked to the galley. I did not walk the deck, for I could not face food. Worried that I had not eaten, the crew offered to take food to me, but I was not hungry and assured them I would be fine. Although the gale eased in late morning, fog developed. The captain said he had lost so much time because of storm and fog that he would not go to the Iceland herring grounds but to Faeroe. Without radar, however, he could not move into Faeroe because of fog, so we waited, dropping speed just enough to meet the bigger waves safely. Consequently we tossed like a cork for hours, despite lesser seas.

Feast below Higravtind, Magnar Pettersen on right, 23 July 1950

Svolværgeita from the steep ridge behind, July 1950

31 July. Klakksvik on Faeroe

The boat still tossed, but I had become used to it and managed to take biscuits and tea in the galley. Also the biggest waves had become smaller, so it was safer to make a run for it along the deck, between one big wave and the next. At midday, clouds still hung low with showers, but the fog suddenly lifted so we could begin to move at full speed. In late afternoon we saw Faeroe, a dark wall of huge sea-cliffs and terraced broad hills wreathed in mist and rain. As we approached, the swell eased and I enjoyed eating a big meal in the galley along with most of the crew and the captain. The captain said he would go to Klakksvik to buy supplies, and though almost no boats went from Faeroe to Iceland, Aberdeen trawlers often used Klakksvik, so I should easily get a boat home.

In early evening we moved up a fjord between steep hills to a village at the top, Klakksvik. The steep grassy hills had terraces of volcanic rock. Many sheep grazed, and on gentle lower slopes stood small farms with fields of hay, grass and potatoes. As we berthed, I saw along the quay a small old Aberdeen trawler, the *Kinellar*!

I walked over and asked for the skipper. A crewman ushered me to a room with a big table and many charts. The silver-haired sharp-eyed skipper asked me to sit. Recognising his Buchan voice, I used the Buchan speech of north-east Scots for the first time in a month. After asking where I had been, he offered to take me to Aberdeen at no cost and would leave in an hour. He had a full load of fish after a month off Greenland and Iceland, and had called at Klakksvik to buy supplies including ice for the fish, and to repair the engine.

Svolvær from east wall of Svolværgjeita, 24 July 1950

Now I returned to the *Staursund* for my bag and thanked her captain. Most of the crew had vanished into the village. Then I transferred to the *Kinellar*, where my sleeping quarters had far more space than in the *Staursund*. In the *Staursund's* tiny galley we had to stand while eating, or else carry the meal to the foc'sle. The *Kinellar* had a galley where ten men could sit. On the other hand, as I expected, toilet and washing facilities in the tiny Norwegian boat far surpassed those in the larger but older *Kinellar*. The *Kinellar* crew said the boat had no toilet, so "you piss on the deck and shite in the coal". They shovelled the coal into the furnace for the engine that drove the boat.

Shortly we left, to shouts and waves from the *Staursund*. As we steamed out of the fjord, the skipper asked me to the chart room for tea, where most of the crew had already gathered. While we drank big mugs of hot strong tea and ate warm bread freshly baked by the cook, the skipper set a course for the western end of the Pentland Firth off Orkney. Then he asked me about my trip. When I said I had caught salmon to eat, he cringed slightly. Later, a deckhand told me that the skipper, mate and the fishermen hailed from Inverallochy, Cairnbulg and St Combs near Fraerburgh, where strict religion held sway. Taboo words included salmon, to be called red fish, pig (porker), and minister (sky pilot). They owned the boat and shared the profits, whereas the waged deckhands were Aberdonians.

As dusk fell we reached open sea and the boat tumbled. Normally I would have been sick, but I had become used to it and felt fine. The cook served Scotch broth with lumps of Faeroe mutton, along with warm

Pinnacle of Svolværgjeita from harbour below, 24 July 1950

AW looks out of bridge of Aberdeen trawler Kinellar south of Faeroe, 1 August 1950

bread and butter, followed by boiled haddock caught by the crew and boiled potatoes bought at Klakksvik. A meal fit for kings, I thought.

1 August. South from Faeroe on an Aberdeen trawler

I awoke to find a slight swell and bright sun. The deckhands said breakfast would soon be ready and I fell upon it. First came porridge in north-east Scots style with salt in the water, raw oatmeal sprinkled on top, and fresh milk bought at Klakksvik and served in a separate mug, and then tea and hot butteries freshly baked by the cook.

Soon I sensed discord in the crew. The engineer did not wish the engine to run at full speed because only temporary repairs had been done. The skipper wanted to reach Aberdeen quickly so that the fish would be in good condition and fetch a high price. Meanwhile the log that registers the distance travelled had broken, so nobody knew how far we had gone. The engineer and deckhands thought the skipper had tampered with the log at night. The log still floated behind, attached by a wire to the stern of the boat.

Anyway, as a result we felt uncertain as we looked for Orkney ahead. Despite bright sunshine, a heavy haze blurred the sea, with mirage-like conditions due to refraction. On several occasions someone shouted "Land ahead" but soon it would vanish. The boat moved far more slowly than it could, but the engineer said it would be crazy to go faster because the engine might be seriously damaged and might even blow up. At this the skipper shook his head and said little, other than that we were dead on course, and those who did not believe it could check for themselves by looking at the sun.

2 August. Past Orkney

Next day, again sunny, we saw Orkney far away, this time real. At night, lighthouses flashed. We came through the Pentland Firth with fairly smooth tide-races, running like vast slow rivers.

3 August. To Aberdeen

Off the north-east tip of Caithness in the morning, the skipper set course for Kinnaird Head at Fraserburgh. Then we relaxed in warm sun, with little wind and a sparkling silver sea. Gradually a fog developed. At noon we should have seen Kinnaird Head, but saw only thin fog under sunshine and blue sky. Suddenly big vertical cliffs loomed out of the fog, stretching for miles. "Faar's this?" (Where's this?) said a deckhand. Nobody knew, except me! Since I had been 16, I had cycled to the Troup and Pennan cliffs to count sea-birds, and now recognised their every detail. I explained this on the chart to the skipper and he turned east.

In early afternoon and now out of the fog, we rounded Kinnaird Head and passed Cairnbulg, Inverallochy and St Combs. Here the skipper steered the boat close inshore, hooted its horn, and blew clouds of white steam from its chimney. Scores of people in the villages ran to the shore, where they waved blankets and mats, shouting and whistling. The fishermen on the *Kinellar* responded likewise. An Aberdonian deckhand shook his head, telling me this was daft tribalism.

The skipper swung out to sea again and continued along the coast to Aberdeen. I noticed Bennachie and Clachnaben, appearing far bigger than Lochnagar and the Cairngorms. I recalled the old rhyme 'Clochnaben and Bennachie, are twa landmarks fae the sea'. As we passed the breakwater of Aberdeen harbour, a man with a loud-hailer in a little hut asked where we had come from. "Greenland" shouted the skipper impressively.

We berthed at Aberdeen in late evening and prepared to unload the fish. Most deckhands went home or to pubs. The skipper advised me to sleep on the boat, because it would be too late to make arrangements with my father in Turriff, and a watchman would guard the boat overnight. He shook hands warmly, and I said "Thanks, skipper, for takkin me back". He replied "I wis glaid to help a Buchan lad and it wis fine hearin aboot your adventures". Then he was off northwards in a smart black car driven by a relative.

4 August. At Aberdeen fish market

I woke to the din of screaming gulls and loud banging as fish were unloaded. Breakfast I ate in the market cafe, excellent porridge and tea with a hot roll. One of the *Kinellar*'s crew gave me a big lump of Greenland halibut to take

Aberdeen harbour in the morning, 4 August 1950

home. When I phoned home, my father said he was to come to Aberdeen in the afternoon to meet Alex Leggatt, who farmed near Turriff and had just retired.

Later, in Union Street I met my father at a cafe where we had afternoon tea. Then we walked to the Athenaeum restaurant, where Alex treated us to a beer and an excellent dinner with friendly waiters. It all seemed unreal to me. My father drove us to the quay, where I collected my pack and ice-axe from the *Kinellar* and then showed him and Alex round the empty boat on a warm sunny evening. We arrived late at Turriff. Next day my father drove with me to Braemar, and my diary noted 'the hills seemed to have fallen backwards' after the steep rock spires of Lofoten.

Chapter 12. Late 1950

9 August. Corrour to Loch Avon

After Stewart and I had fished at Poll an Eisg all morning, in the afternoon he left Corrour Bothy for Luibeg and home, while I went over Ben Macdui. A westerly gale rose as I climbed Coire Clach nan Taillear, tricky on the boulders. The gale blew me off boulders several times, and once near the top a severe gust lifted me up off a boulder for a second. Big spots of rain fell from black clouds and mist, and utter gloom prevailed in the great hole of Loch Avon. A middle-aged Swiss couple on holiday had decided to stay the night at the Shelter Stone. As I arrived they were trying vainly to make a fire out of wet blaeberry bushes for a drum-up of tea, so I boiled water for them on my stove. At dusk, clouds raced across the sky, the black mass of the Sticil crag glistened with water, and waterfalls and wild winds roared. The Swiss were delighted. "This is the loneliest, most beautiful place we have ever seen", they said.

10 August. From the Shelter Stone to Luibeg

The gale was stronger, with some gusts that blew water spindrift off Loch Avon for hundreds of feet to meet the hurrying low clouds. I cooked breakfast of fried trout for all three of us, with tea. The Swiss wrote an entry in the visitors' book "We met AW, a very cultivated troglodyte. He gave us fried trouts better than in the Five Arms Hotel, Braemar". Bidding them goodbye, I left and nearby saw a hen ptarmigan with a big chick. At almost 3000 feet, water spindrift off Loch Avon rose for over 700 feet, above me. Beside Loch Etchachan, the strongest gusts tore out moss and flung it past as I crouched low to avoid being blown off my feet, a very rough day. I descended into Glen Derry and so to Luibeg.

13 October. To Luibeg

From Turriff I took a bus to Aberdeen, left kit at my new lodgings ready for university on the 17th, caught a bus to Braemar and walked to Luibeg in the late evening. Next day Bob and I strolled round his fox traps in Glen Derry. Rowan leaves here are flaring red, but with less frost at Braemar are only golden. In the evening Bob and I walked to shoot rabbits in lower Glen Derry and got one each. I saw a salmon parr stranded in a shallow tributary. Bob says they introduced 40 salmon from Clunie to Lui this year and he hopes they will spawn. The salmon ladder in Glen Lui has been completed.

15 October. Ben Macdui

A wild south-west wind blew, with cloud. I walked up Glen Luibeg, seeing at the bridge a sick old stag which still had velvet on its antlers. Below Coire an Lochan Uaine I made a fire with dead pine branches and drummed up a pot of tea. Then I walked up to Lochan Uaine which lay in great shelter. After crossing into Coire Sputan Dearg I climbed one of the spouts (wide gullies). Above, fresh snow lay up to a foot deep, partly above old snow from last week's storm. Four golden plover were at the Sappers' Bothy and two cock ptarmigan at the summit. Suddenly the mist cleared, revealing wild views of Braeriach.

As I descended to Loch Etchachan, sunlight broke through to sparkle on the new snow, a fine sight after a few months without seeing fresh snow. To the north-east the sky was blue and the Moray Firth brilliant in sunshine. Warm plum colours and hard-cut blue cloud shadows moved over the moors beyond Glen Avon. Past Loch Etchachan, the bluest I have ever seen, I descended to Glen Derry. Stags and hinds stood thickly on the west slope half way down, and tawny owls hooted as I neared Derry Lodge before dusk.

31 December. A lone ski-tour on the Monadh Liath on a perfect day

On the evening of the 30th, Dad, Mum and I went to Newtonmore, and tomorrow Dad has to go on a business trip. Tom Weir, Douglas Scott and some other Glasgow SMC members come tomorrow night to see in the New Year.

By morning, not a cloud broke a cloudless sky. I walked up the road to Glen Banchor with rising hope, for deep snow lay above 1200 feet and drifts of frozen snow stretched far below. Hoar frost sparkled on the heather. After walking up the old field by Allt a' Chaorainn, I put on my skis with skins and soon reached the red bothy. Grouse cackled on this fine morning, and the wide Coire Dubh behind the bothy gleamed with a brilliant silvery white light in the strong sun. It was a ski-tourer's dream. I could point the skis uphill in a straight line to the top of A' Chailleach far above.

At the cairn I removed my skis and sat on them while eating sandwiches. The sun felt warm. Although only a few days had passed since the shortest day, brilliant sparkling light shone on many miles of snowy hills to the south, and the edges of ice and frozen snow on cliffs and lochs gleamed bright silver. Not a breath of wind stirred. Down in the strath a blue haze indicated a temperature inversion, with smoke caught in a layer near the ground. The world seemed at peace.

Dozing, I slept a few minutes. I turned to look over the huge tablelands of the Monadh Liath, today stretching in unsullied white as far as the eye could see towards Inverness and Fort Augustus. Beyond, the snowy peaks of the north-west Highlands rose sharp and clear under a blue sky, their southern slopes shining in the sun. Away towards the Atlantic, a grey band of high cloud indicated an approaching front, still many hours away.

Removing the skins, I skied in zigzags down the fairly steep slope to the north-west, and then poled easily up the gentle gradient to Carn Sgulain. It gave an even better closer view of the snowy plateau falling gently to Abhainn Cro Chlach and other tributaries of Findhorn. From Carn Sgulain a broken sheep fence runs east to the little top of Am Bodach. The slope to the south, usually a good ski-run, excelled on this fine afternoon. In great swoops I whirled down over sparkling powder where the bright light showed every slight change in the snow's surface. Contouring west of Am Bodach, I skied above the rocks of Bruthach an Easain, festooned in snow and ice.

Another fine run followed south-east to the Geal Charn, which I skirted on its west side to continue along the fence to Beinn Bhuidhe. Now there came the best run of the day, for more than a mile south to the green bothy. I could point the skis in any direction south, west or east, and run straight downhill or in long sweeping traverses. The floor of the glen came visibly closer as I swooped down. At the green bothy I stopped for a moment to remove my skis and walk inside, and then out into afternoon sunshine. For the next mile I kept the skis on, at first down the path on the east side of the burn, and then over a moor with frozen pools and lochans. This led to a birch wood where frozen snow lay below the trees, and finally to the farm above Glen Road in the village, where I took my skis off and shouldered them down the street.

New Year's Day and following days brought low cloud, wind, thaw and moist snowfall. We found some quite good downhill skiing on a short steep gully at Drumochter, but to me it seemed almost tedious after that brilliant day on the Monadh Liath. That tour showed how good a day can be for weather and snow, and yet how short this sometimes lasts, with poor weather on days before and after. One has to leap at good opportunities, for they may not last. Even half an hour of a good tour can surpass many days of average or poor conditions, and bring far more joy and wonder.

Bibliography

Watson, A. (2011). It's a fine day for the hill. Paragon Publishing, Rothersthorpe.

Some other books by the author

1963. Mountain hares. Sunday Times Publications, London (by AW & R. Hewson)

1970. Animal populations in relation to their food resources (Editor). Blackwell Scientific Publications, Oxford and Edinburgh

1974. The Cairngorms, their natural history and scenery. Collins, London, and 1981 Melven Press, Perth (by D. Nethersole-Thompson & AW)

1975. The Cairngorms. Scottish Mountaineering Club District Guide, published by Scottish Mountaineering Trust. Second edition published 1992

1976. Grouse management. The Game Conservancy, Fordingbridge, and the Institute of Terrestrial Ecology, Huntingdon (by AW & G.R. Miller)

1982. Animal population dynamics. Chapman and Hall, London and New York (by R. Moss, AW & J. Ollason)

1982. The future of the Cairngorms. The North East Mountain Trust, Aberdeen (by K. Curry-Lindahl, AW & D. Watson)

1984. The place names of upper Deeside. Aberdeen University Press (by AW & E. Allan)

1998. The Cairngorms of Scotland. Eagle Crag, Aberdeen (by S. Rae & AW)

2008. Grouse: the grouse species of Britain and Ireland. Collins, London, New Naturalist Library No 107 (by AW & R. Moss)

2010. Cool Britannia: snowier times in 1580–1930 than since. Paragon Publishing, Rothersthorpe (by AW & I. Cameron)

2011. It's a fine day for the hill. Paragon Publishing, Rothersthorpe

2011. A zoologist on Baffin Island, 1953. Paragon Publishing, Rothersthorpe

2011. Vehicle hill tracks in northern Scotland. The North East Mountain Trust, Aberdeen, published imprint Paragon Publishing, Rothersthorpe

2011. A snow book, northern Scotland: based on the author's field observations in 1938–2011. Paragon Publishing, Rothersthorpe

Author

Adam Watson, BSc, PhD, DSc, DUniv, raised in lowland Aberdeenshire, is a retired research ecologist aged 81. Lifelong interests on winter snow began in 1937, snow patches in 1938, the Cairngorms in 1939. A mountaineer and ski-mountaineer since boyhood, he experienced Scotland, Iceland, Norway, Sweden, mainland Canada, Newfoundland, Baffin Island, Finland, Switzerland, Italy, Vancouver Island and Alaska. His main research was on population biology, behaviour and habitat of northern birds and mammals. In retirement he contributed many scientific papers on these topics and 17 papers and two books on snow patches. He is a Fellow of the Arctic Institute of North America, Centre for Ecology and Hydrology, Royal Meteorological Society, Royal Society of Edinburgh, and Society of Biology, and an Emeritus Member of the Ecological Society of North America. An Honorary Life Member of the Cairngorm Club, Scottish Ornithologists' Club, and Worldwide Fund for Nature, since 1954 he has been a member of the Scottish Mountaineering Club and since 1968 author of the Club's District Guide to the Cairngorms.

Lightning Source UK Ltd.
Milton Keynes UK
UKOW06f1039181213

223231UK00003B/7/P